TESTIMONY

TESTIMONY

WRITERS OF THE WEST SPEAK ON BEHALF OF UTAH WILDERNESS

COMPILED BY
STEPHEN TRIMBLE
TERRY TEMPEST WILLIAMS

Distributed by Publishers Group West
Published 1996 by Milkweed Editions
Printed in the United States of America
Cover design by Sally Wagner
Literature for a Land Ethic illustration by Betsy Bowen
Interior design by Will Powers
Interior maps by Nancy Wirsig McClure, Hand to Mouse Arts
The text of this book is set in Minion.
96 97 98 99 00   5 4 3 2 1
First Edition

Milkweed Editions is a not-for-profit publisher. We gratefully acknowledge support from the Elmer A. Anderson Foundation; Belford Foundation; James Ford Bell Foundation; the Bush Foundation; Wallace and Mary Lee Dayton; Target Stores, Dayton's, and Mervyn's by the Dayton Hudson Foundation; Ecolab Foundation; General Mills Foundation; Give to the Earth Foundation: Honeywell Foundation; Jerome Foundation; Marbrook Foundation; The McKnight Foundation; Andrew W. Mellon Foundation; Kathy Stevens Dougherty and Michael E. Dougherty Fund of the Minneapolis Foundation; Minnesota State Arts Board through an appropriation by the Minnesota State Legislature; Challenge and Literature Programs of the National Endowment for the Arts; Kate and Stuart Nielsen; The Lawrence M. and Elizabeth Ann O'Shaughnessy Charitable Income Trust in honor of Lawrence M. O'Shaughnessy; Piper Jaffray Companies, Inc.; Ritz Foundation on behalf of Mr. and Mrs. E. J. Phelps, Jr.; John and Beverly Rollwagen Fund of the Minneapolis Foundation; The St. Paul Companies, Inc.; Star Tribune/ Cowles Media Foundation; Elly and Sheldon Sturgis; Surdna Foundation; James R. Thorpe Foundation; U. S. West Foundation; Lila Wallace-Reader's Digest Literary Publishers Marketing Development Program, funded through a grant to the Council of Literary Magazines and Presses; and generous individuals.

Library of Congress Cataloging-in-Publication Data

Testimony : writers of the West speak on behalf of Utah wilderness /
    compiled by Stephen Trimble and Terry Tempest Williams.
        p.   cm.
    ISBN 1-57131-212-9 (paper)
    1. Wilderness areas—Utah.   2. Environmental policy—United
States.   3. Nature conservation—Philosophy.   I. Trimble, Stephen,
1950–   .   II. Williams, Terry Tempest.
QH76.5.U8T47   1996
333.78′216′09792—dc20   96–17647
                                                                    CIP

This book is printed on recycled, acid-free paper.

For the Moon-Eyed Horse

Testimony

Something will have gone out of us as a people
if we ever let the remaining wilderness be destroyed.

WALLACE STEGNER
"Wilderness Letter"
1960

Testimony

An Act of Faith

T O B E A R T E S T I M O N Y is to bear witness; we speak from the truth of our lives. How do we put our love for the land into action? This book is one model, an act of faith by writers who believe in the power of story, a bedrock reminder of how wild nature continues to inform, inspire, and sustain us.

In the summer of 1995, debate over the fate of Utah's wildlands reached a climax. At issue: agreeing on acreage and boundaries for congressionally designated wilderness within the 22 million acres of Utah administered by the U. S. Bureau of Land Management (BLM). The Utah delegation, uniformly conservative for the first time in many years, placed the "Utah Public Lands Management Act" before Congress, calling for only 1.8 million acres of wilderness. In its details, this bill undermined the integrity of the 1964 Wilderness Act. Its unprecedented "hard release" language opened up undesignated lands for development and allowed gas pipelines, communication towers, and dams within congressionally designated wilderness.

As naturalists, writers, and citizens living in Salt Lake City, we became deeply involved with this issue. After a round of public hearings that made clear the Utah delegation was beyond reason, we imagined another approach, some path behind the normal barriers that, together, as writers, we might travel.

For inspiration, we looked to the afternoon in 1960 when Wallace Stegner wrote a letter to David Pesonen of the Outdoor Recreation Resources Review Commission to address "the wilderness *idea*, which is a resource in itself." Seated at his desk in the hills above Palo Alto, Stegner imagined the view across his boyhood haunts in southern Utah. He called these lands "the geography of hope."

This letter has become a timeless statement of the nature of American wilderness. A quote from Stegner's letter appears as the epigraph for *Testimony:* "Something will have gone out of us as a people if we ever let the remaining wilderness be destroyed."

In early August 1995, we sent a letter to twenty-five writers who have Utah's redrock sand and alkali dust in their souls, writers of the West even if they do not live in the West. We asked them to donate a short piece for a chapbook that we would place on the desk of every representative and senator. We imagined we could communicate to members of Congress who have never seen Utah's wildlands why these places are unique; why they matter so much to all Americans, whether they live in Alabama, Minnesota, or New York; and why a seemingly huge acreage of nearly two million acres is completely inadequate.

"We believe," we wrote in this letter, that "these essays can make a difference by elevating the level of discussion to one of soulful contemplation on behalf of all lands in North America, their spiritual value, their psychological as well as biological necessity."

Miraculously, three weeks later, we had nineteen essays in hand—seventeen of them original pieces. To these responses to our letter, we added a piece by Tom Lyon, his testimony from the citizens hearing on June 22, 1995, in Salt Lake City, and a poem by Richard Shelton—a poem about the loss of Glen Canyon under Lake Powell, a mirror of the stakes in the current discussion.

Our colleagues, the twenty-one men and women in *Testimony*, belong to a community of writers who honor the land. They range in age from Margaret Murie (B. 1902) to Rick Bass (B. 1958). The old axiom "write what you know" is true. These writers know these places and they love them. They understand the imperative of wildness.

They argue for greater acreage and stronger protection. They do not make their arguments as political diatribes. These essays and poems celebrate the importance of

5

wilderness to individuals and to American culture. They are personal testimonies.

President Bill Clinton has called these public lands "our common ground." We believe him.

We took care to remain free of ties to any political party or environmental organization. We wanted to speak as independent voices, to avoid dismissal as producers of one more piece of propaganda.

And so we obtained a commitment from Annette and Ian Cumming of the Utah-based Cumming Foundation to pay for printing and design. With a grant of just under $6,000, we remained sovereign, writers addressing Congress personally. We printed 1,000 copies for distribution to all members of Congress, to the conservation community, and to the press. We chose to make *Testimony* a limited resource, like wilderness.

With extraordinary serendipity, the book came together quickly and smoothly. A week of light editing and follow-up with authors, a week in design, a week in printing—and we had a book. With *Testimony* in hand, we flew to Washington, D. C., for a press conference at the Triangle in front of the United States Capitol on September 27, 1995. Tom Watkins joined us at the podium, placing the project in historic and national perspective. Representatives Maurice Hinchey (D-NY) and Bruce Vento (D-MN) responded, accepting *Testimony* on behalf of their colleagues and distributing the book to each member of the House with a cover letter. Senator Russell Feingold (D-WI) subsequently sponsored *Testimony* in the Senate and sent the book to his colleagues with a similar letter.

After the press conference, a journalist asked "What will you do if this book makes no difference, if no one listens?"

"Writers never know the effect of their words," we responded. "We write as an act of faith."

We still have much work to do. We trust that the publication of *Testimony* by Milkweed Editions will carry these ideas forward and that the spirit of this book will rouse people to take action on behalf of their own homelands. We believe in the power of story to bypass political rhetoric and pierce the heart.

We live in the geography of hope.

STEPHEN TRIMBLE   TERRY TEMPEST WILLIAMS
1 April 1996
Salt Lake City, Utah

Introduction

Bearing Witness

MORE THAN ONE HUNDRED AND TWENTY YEARS AGO, a group of acolytes wanted to persuade the Congress of the United States to designate the region of the Upper Yellowstone a national park—the first to be made strictly because of the unique character and beauty of the land itself. It might have seemed an impossible hope; this was, after all, the beginning of the period characterized by historian Vernon L. Parrington as "The Great Barbecue," when the resources of the West were exploited to a cheerful fare-thee-well, full speed ahead and damn the tomorrows. Furthermore, most of those in Congress, and indeed the country, hardly knew that this great wild place existed, much less comprehended its magnificence as landscape.

What did the park supporters do? They took scientific evidence, lyrical descriptions, and—above all—the stunningly powerful photographs of William Henry Jackson and the lush paintings of Thomas Moran, both of whom had been to the Upper Yellowstone with the government exploring expedition of Ferdinand Hayden, and combined them into a packet of information that they waved in the faces of presumably amazed and astounded senators and representatives until the lawmakers did the right thing: Yellowstone National Park.

The writers and artists involved had borne witness to the glory of a little-known place. So do those in this small book celebrating southern Utah. It is a different age, now, and we are not naive enough to think that most of those in the present Contract on America Congress will gasp in wonder at the images and testimony given here, however powerful and persuasive they may be, and, like their nineteenth-century counterparts, spring into action to save the threatened Utah wilderness. But we do hope that this expression of love will cause the more thoughtful members of Congress to stop for a moment and consider just what is at stake here—and the fact that what the American people lose if we sacrifice common sense to the transient ambitions of a few will be gone, for all intents and purposes, forever. What if, members might ask themselves, Congress had not moved to protect Yellowstone?

Let's get to some of the hardware then. The lands that are enfolded in the generic term "Utah Wilderness" as we use it here are the most fragile and beautiful and ecologically significant areas embraced within the 22 million acres of Utah land administered by the Bureau of Land Management and held in trust by that agency for the American people—all the people. These special areas include the volcanic peaks of the Henry Mountains, rising improbably but sublimely from the red desert roof of the Colorado Plateau. They include the twisting rambles of Muddy Creek, cutting its serpentine way through the headwaters country of the San Rafael River. They include the riparian treasures of the Dirty Devil River, the Escalante River, the North Fork of the Virgin; big and little canyon complexes with names like Labyrinth, Parunuweap, Westwater, Arch, Mule, Carcass, Cheesebox; mesas called Bridger Jack, Square Top, Wild Horse, Tarantula, Sams, Sewemup; there are the North Wah Wahs, Little Goose Creek, Hurricane Wash, Fiftymile Mountain, Papoose Canyon, the Studhorse Peaks, the Silver Island Mountains, Fortknocker Canyon, Cave Point, Behind the Rocks; there are hidden springs and pools and creeks, miniature waterfalls, distance, aridity, complexity, sky, beauty . . .

The conservation community—specifically, The Wilderness Society, the Southern Utah Wilderness Alliance, and the thirty-four other local, regional, and national groups that make up the Utah Wilderness Coalition—would like to save these and scores of other wilderness enclaves of southern Utah in America's Redrock Wilderness Act, HR 1500, which would add 5.7 million acres of them to the National Wilderness Preservation System. Seventy percent of Utah's citizens also want the vast majority of these threatened wild places protected.

What is threatening these lands? A roundup of the usual suspects would include mining, grazing, timber extraction, oil and gas development, industrial-strength tourism, and unfettered urban growth and the water projects that will be necessary to sustain it. Why do we need to worry about all this with special concern now? Because the Utah congressional delegation has promised to pursue its own wilderness legislation—HR 1745 in the House; S 884 in the Senate—even though it was beaten back on the first attempt in March 1996. The delegation's proposed "Utah Public Lands Management Act" is a hammer aimed at the undeveloped heart of Utah. First, it would designate only 1.8 million acres as wilderness, limiting such designations to areas in which no one has or is ever likely to have any economic interest. It is the desert equivalent of the "rocks and ice" wilderness designations the U. S. Forest Service used in the 1960s and 1970s as it struggled to obviate the Wilderness Act of 1964 by keeping most lower-altitude forests, grasslands, rivers, and other potentially "valuable" resources out of the wilderness hopper. Second, the two delegation bills would release all remaining Bureau of Land Management lands in Utah from any future consideration as wilderness, ever. Most of these lands would be opened immediately to any kind of economic development that seemed feasible or tempting, no matter how destructive to the land or the human communities in it.

Consider some very likely possibilities in the area of energy production alone: enormous tar sands mining developments on the edge of Glen Canyon National Recreation Area and in the Book Cliffs; a 3,000 megawatt coal-burning power plant in the heart of the Kaiparowits Plateau; coal strip mining south and west of Bryce Canyon National Park; a petroleum and carbon dioxide gas extraction field in the headwaters of the Escalante River, involving as many as ninety-seven production wells and eleven four-story compressor plants; and to support these industrial explosions, hundreds of miles of new roads and thousands of miles of electric lines and pipelines, the construction of brand-new towns to house workers and service their needs, the grotesque distension of existing towns, and rivers dammed to furnish water for industrial and domestic use.

Add to this scenario the prospect of thousands of acres of native pinyon and juniper forests being "chained" out of existence so that cattle-friendly grasses can be planted, of biologically rich riparian areas being trampled into ruin by those same cattle, of the last of the timber being stripped from the mountains, and of the rise of elaborate Disney-like resort and recreation complexes, and you have the kind of bleak, nightmarish vision of a burned-out future that can drive even "nonpolitical" folk like poets into paroxysms of anger and sadness.

There is an abundance of both emotions in the poetry and prose of this book, as there should be. Anger and sadness are touchstones of passion, and to save these lands from the worst that could happen to them—and to give them the best that it is in our human power to give—is going to require passion, and plenty of it.

In the canyon country of southern Utah, as everywhere else, we must learn, finally, that wilderness is not, as our history has insisted, a threat to be conquered but, in fact, a protection to be embraced. For in wilderness, as in the eyes of the wild creatures that inhabit it, we find something that binds us firmly to the long history of life on Earth, something that can teach us how to live on this cooling cinder of a planet, how to accept our limitations, how to celebrate the love we feel when we let ourselves feel it for all other living creatures.

When voting on the Utah wilderness bill, the Congress of the United States has the opportunity to demonstrate this connection and commitment more profoundly than at any time since passage of the Wilderness Act itself. What better talisman could we have for the future of wilderness preservation as we race toward the end of one century and the beginning of another?

T. H. WATKINS
(B. 1936)

named finally on the American maps after a Spaniard
who never saw it but was first in a century of European
exploration of the sandrock country. A century of horses
    kicking
stones down cliffs; of hungry men huddled around the
    delicate,
aromatic heat of sagebrush fires; of curses flung at boulder
choked defiles, sheer ridges, terrain less hospitable
than the treacherous, endless seas.

The maps were drawn; meticulous traceries revealing
routes, obstacles, dead ends, naming them, bringing
the country into chart rooms and libraries, spelling
its topography out to the curious eyes of scholars,
politicians, prospectors, to itinerant farmers
bent on finding water and a patch of soil.

Still, the Unknown was not domesticated, being too
    recalcitrant
for that, too sparse, too fierce for more than a few crazies
to ever settle, no matter how they appeared at the least
rumor of riches; digging up whole river banks, hauling in

cables stouter than their forearms, chiseling
initials on sandstone.

                    Now, hikers with fifty-pound packs
scramble over boulders, ford a thigh-deep river
looking for miracles.

All this sweat notwithstanding, the secrets hold.
The shadows are not plumbed yet, nor the springs traced
to their cool hearts.

The Unknown is traveled but not penetrated, studied
but not deciphered, mapped but not squared.

Ann Weiler Walka, Itinerant Poet, 1993

The country here is almost entirely solid sand rock, high
hills and mountains cut all to pieces by deep gulches
which are in many places altogether impassible. It is cer-
tainly the worst country I ever saw.

Platte D. Lyman, Hole-in-the-Rock pioneer, 1879

Back to field-test my poem about the Escalante, I'm hiking
down to the river from Forty Mile Ridge, a layover camp
for the Hole-in-the-Rockers. A maze of sandstone spalls
off from the end of the red dirt road; pink swells, curious
twists of shadow, patinated walls that sheer into canyons
like sheets of rain.

    John Wesley Powell's men mapped the Unknown River

only a few years before Platte Lyman led 250 of the faithful across this precipitous country in wagons. Powell admired the Mormons' knack for making a living in thirsty, stony landscapes, but even they didn't settle here. In 1934, when the unclaimed lands between Canada and Mexico became a public trust to be managed by the Bureau of Land Management, 22 million un-proved-up acres of Utah, most of them as intimidating as this place, were included.

Two generations after the Taylor Grazing Act, we still envision traditional ways to make a silk purse out of sand and rock—grazing, mining, hunting, wood cutting, recreation. None of those endeavors except recreation has come to much; 5 million acres of Utah's public land haven't even invited a graded road.

Why not acknowledge that there is something here more important to our beleaguered society than a marginal mine, an overgrazed permit? A great American myth is embodied in wild lands, and it is myth, ultimately, that holds a people together.

The bits of this continent too formidable to penetrate by road hold the last of what drew our ancestors to North America, be it ten or ten thousand years ago, an opportunity to breathe deep and re-imagine their lives. These scraps of Eden still afford us awe in an age of cynicism, steady us when human affairs are dizzyingly complicated, reaffirm our eroding sense of American innocence and courage. Places like these, places to get lost, to become grounded, to meet our Maker, to rediscover our forebears' resourcefulness and grit, to take heart, are promised in our most abiding stories.

Looking out over this lovely wasteland I think of Africa and what it has lost in my lifetime; the great herds, the vast seas of grass, wildness going fast as a population explodes into the industrial age. Surely a rich and prudent country like mine would never let its last reserves of land dwindle into token parks, too meager and trampled to be vital. To sacrifice our last empty places to human affairs is to admit to ourselves that our backs are against the wall.

The rich blue mystery of the American continent, the dreamscape that harbors bears and cougars and mud-breathing fishes, informs and nurtures our collective soul. Settlers must have nodded ruefully when a Salt Lake paper reported that this wilderness was good for nothing except to hold the world together. In fact, it does exactly that.

ANN WEILER WALKA

(B. 1941)

My place of refuge is a wilderness canyon in southern Utah.

Its scale is exactly right. Smooth curves of sandstone embrace and cradle me. From the road, I cross a mile of slickrock to reach the stream. This creek runs year-round, banked by orchids and ferns. Entering the tangle of greenery, I rediscover paradise. The canyon is a secret, a power spot, a place of pilgrimage.

I found this canyon in my youth, twenty years ago. I came here again and again. I brought special friends and lovers. When my wife and I met and I discovered she knew this place, I felt certain she knew a place deep within me as well. My children are within a year of walking into the canyon on their own. I thrill to think of that first visit with them.

On those early trips, I rarely saw other people. Once, in the velvet light before dawn, I awoke, sat bolt upright, and looked past my sleeping bag into a lone ponderosa pine — a tree that brought the spicy scent of mountain forest to this desert canyon. A few seconds later, a great horned owl noiselessly landed on a branch and looked back at me with fierce eyes. The owl flew downcanyon, searching for unwary mice. I lay back, fell asleep, and awoke again when the sun warmed me.

I bathed in plunge pools and waded along the stream, learning to pay attention, looking for reflections and leaf patterns and rock forms to photograph—details I would not see if the canyon had not taught me to look. Never before had I spent so much time alone on the land. Here, I matured, as a naturalist and photographer and as a human being.

This wilderness canyon made me whole. It still can restore me to wholeness when the stress of my life pulls me thin. It bestows peace of mind that lasts for months.

People smile when they remember such particular places on the earth where the seasons and textures and colors belong to them. Where they know, with assurance and precision, the place and their relationship to it.

"This is my garden."

"This is our family beach."

"I know this grove like the back of my hand."

"I can tell you where every fish in this stream hides."

"I remember this view; it takes me back to my childhood."

These landscapes nourish and teach and heal. They help keep us sane, they give us strength, they connect us to our roots in the earth, they remind us that we share in the flow of life and death. We encounter animals in their native place and they look into our eyes with the amalgam of indifference and companionship that separates us from and unites us with other creatures. A garden can connect us with wildness. Wilderness connects us with our ancestral freedoms even more powerfully.

Recently, we visited a canyon new to us in the southern Utah wilderness, this time with urban cousins—two girls, seven and eleven. The younger girl shrieked with delight as she splashed along the stream. The older girl spotted a whipsnake, a nesting Cooper's hawk, beetles, Indian paintbrush. We painted ourselves with golden cattail pollen and launched boats we wove from rushes and milkweed leaves. Taught to never walk alone in their city, here the girls forged ahead out of sight, exploring, appropriating power, gathering the dependable certainties of the wilderness, building emotional bedrock, new layers of confidence and self-esteem. Perhaps this canyon will become their canyon.

We need to preserve every chance to have such experiences, for ourselves, our children, and the grandchildren of our grandchildren.

For we have reached the end of the gold rush. This wild country is our home, not simply one more stop on the way to the next boomtown. Respect for our home, thinking as natives, begins in our backyards, with our children. We move outward from there to local parks, to preservation of greenbelts, and from there to big wilderness.

The wilderness canyons of Utah belong not to an elite

cadre of backpackers, not to the cattle-raising families of Escalante and Kanab, not to the Utah state legislature, not to the Bureau of Land Management. They belong to all citizens of the United States. In truth, they belong to no one. They are a magnificent expression of the powers of the earth, and we Americans hold Utah wilderness in trust for all humans and all life on our planet.

The truly conservative action becomes clear: to preserve as many wildlands as possible for future generations rather than to fritter them away in casual development. A Utah wilderness bill with too little land preserved and too many exceptions for development is unacceptable, destroying irreplaceable wild places for the short-term wealth of the few.

Every year, our wildlands shrink. We must act now, decisively, boldly. To save my canyon. Their canyon. Your canyon.

We must preserve the wholeness of wild places that belong to everyone and to no one. In doing so, we demonstrate our trustworthiness — our capacity to take a stand on behalf of the land. On behalf of the canyons.

Our canyons.

STEPHEN TRIMBLE
(B. 1950)

Forget for a moment the politics of wilderness. Forget all the special interests who have placed their claim on our last remaining untamed lands. Forget the developers, the miners, the ranchers, the oil companies, the urban environmentalists, the scientists, the bikers, hikers, climbers, the hunters, the nature lovers. Forget them all, and as a maker of public policy, think carefully, apart from what any of them want, what you would do if your only criteria were doing what will benefit America in the long run.

We have come to the point in our national development when the pressures of a growing population are about to overwhelm the last remaining wild places in America. Among the most precious of lands at risk are nearly 6 million acres of wilderness in Utah's southern desert. Here, sun, wind, and rain have played with the brilliant, multicolored land for a billion years, leaving the recorded history of the earth's beginnings on a complex landscape of plateaus, cliffs, buttes, and river-cut canyon walls. Here, families in civilizations long gone built their homes in cliff dwellings dug into Navajo Sandstone, raising their children and recording their observations on salmon-red cave walls.

Here, plant and animal live together in the fragile environment of little water, creating a place of perfect balance which, left alone, will thrive for another billion years. Here, it is possible for a human to see like a hawk and believe in magic. Here, we can feel our spiritual connection to the earth challenging us to be better than we are, urging us to reach beyond where we have ever reached before. Here, we can imagine our beginnings and create possibilities for our future. Invading and domesticating this land will permanently change its value, eliminating its contribution to our national psyche and removing an essential element from the national consciousness.

We must save wilderness because in saving it we will be saving part of ourselves. We have been shaped by the wild lands we have lived in, and because they are still part of our landscape, they continue to live within us. When they are gone, many of the fundamental values that created America will also vanish.

At a conscious or subconscious level, America continues to be "the land of the free and the home of the brave" because we can still go to places that are fresh, primitive, and untamed. No one would ever describe France this way. But we think of ourselves as free and brave because we had to be to live in the landscape of our beginning. Wilderness has always fueled our imagination, nurtured our sense of freedom, and kindled our entrepreneurial energies. Without this taproot into our past, we will forget what we have been and may not like what we become. Our relationship with the land has both nurtured and challenged us, giving us those characteristics we consider uniquely American: heartiness, ingenuity, curiosity, toughness under fire, individualism, passion, creativity, warmth, good humor, optimism, and hope.

These attitudes have shaped the American Dream and that dream remains our collective myth, in part, because we can still go and walk on land as it once was everywhere. Take away the wilderness and the American Dream will lose its authenticity. Turn the idea of wilderness into a Disney theme park and watch hope die.

Once when I was visiting the Third Mesa of the Hopi Indians, I spied a tattered sign hanging over the door of a remote trading post. It said, "We don't inherit the earth. We borrow it from our children."

As public policy makers you hold office at a time when you must decide how much of this wild land that nurtured us will pass to future generations. If you decide to domesticate these places, the value they had in shaping our national character will be lost to us forever. Making such a decision would be a tragic mistake. We have used the wilderness to fuel our energy and imagination and to connect us to our spiritual life and our past. Because there was so much of it, we have also consumed the land as fuel for the greatest

25

economy the world has ever known. Now, after only 220 years, the wilderness is almost gone. Now, the argument, of necessity, is not over how much we will use, but how much of what little is left we will save. Hooked as we are on the wish that the environment could be eternally capable of producing on demand, we are tempted to use it all up.

If you forget politics and think only about what's best for our children and grandchildren, you will understand the need to rise above the voices that call for cutting to the last tree, mining until the last hole is dug and abandoned, damming the last remaining free streams, putting roads through the vast silence of the only primitive areas still capable of invoking awe.

If you forget about politics and think about the future, you will follow the sound business practices of any borrower. We are borrowing the land from our children. In the case of wilderness, that which we borrow and use can never be returned. Nor can the contribution its presence makes to the national consciousness, a measurable asset by any calculation, ever be replaced. Instead, we must treat this land as if it were on loan to us, saving it as an endowment for our children. In so doing we ensure that the renewing powers of wilderness will inspire generations to come just as they have inspired us.

The stakes are high. Once the wild places and the wild things that live there are gone, we Americans will lose our sense of uniqueness; we will have no place to go to test our knowledge of ourselves as individuals; and we will watch our genius for discovery atrophy. Wilderness is as American as apple pie—food for our soul. We need all of it that is left, for without it we will surely starve.

KAREN SHEPHERD
(B. 1940)

GLEN CANYON ON THE COLORADO

Past these towering monuments, past these mounded billows
of orange sandstone, past these oak-set glens, past these fern-
decked alcoves, past these mural caves, we glide hour after
hour, stopping now and then, as our attention is arrested by
some new wonder, until we reach a point which is historic.

JOHN WESLEY POWELL

1

soon it will be thirty-five years
since the gamblers passed a leather cup
from hand to hand
some breathing into it for luck
some passing it on quickly
as though it burned

and we said we have been told
it is necessary we said we have waited
long enough let us have
the comfort we deserve and whatever

profit can be earned from it
though it brings darkness
to remote places no one is there

let there be announcements
by those who announce let it be done
let it be over let the rain come
and the water rise
let there be no more talk
of monuments in a distant wilderness
we will create new monuments
to our own ability
we will move over the water
with such speed we will forget
even what we have never known
surely our time has come
let them gather the waters together
and create a lake in the desert
for our pleasure

then we heard the distant
explosions of dice and it was over
that which was reprieved was reprieved
for a while and that which was damned
was damned forever

2

once there was a canyon
where the river was lying down
resting for a while from all its labors
moving in repose past hanging gardens
of ferns and monkey flowers
and sheltered groves of box elders

where in the golden light
of cottonwood and autumn sun
the canyon wren would flirt
with anyone who came along
staying just ahead moving in and out
among polished driftwood and stones
promising something wonderful
around the next bend *follow follow*
she called with a voice as low
and liquid as any siren's song

where sometimes the shadow of a heron
would hoist itself above the water
flapping its wings
as though they needed oiling
while the determined beaver
followed his nose in a straight line
going somewhere important upstream
his silver wake spreading behind him

and at night when the cliffs
seemed to lean inward over the river
like giant black guardians
protecting stone cathedrals from the moon
and the beaver slept in lodges
so close to the surface they could hear
every word the river said
and all that the willows replied
a brilliant ribbon of stars
would unwind itself above the cliffs
following each turn of the canyon walls

soon that place will no longer exist
in the memory of anyone living
and will be hinted at only in photographs
and in the dim visions of words
as untrustworthy as our own

when we say *at this point in time*
to avoid the terror of saying *now*
the unredeemable moment where we live
with all past actions beyond our reach
and sinking down through dark water

3

once there was a canyon
just another canyon on the Colorado
saddest of all the poor
damned rivers of the West
soon it will be thirty-five years
since we passed that point in time
which was historic
since we crossed a dark meridian
from which there is no return

and we drift we drift
on a lake of our own making
casting our offerings upon the water
our cans and bottles
the detritus of careless lives
and we watch our calendars
float away and sink slowly downward
one month at a time into a world
drowned for our good reasons

where a few fish swim
through the ghostly branches
of dead cottonwoods where there is no
season no sunlight on sandstone
no song of the canyon wren nor any sound

where the bones of those
who were not historic
sit under the floors of their houses
in baskets while the stones
of their walls fall silently in
and black silt covers everything

4

where have you gone
bright spirit of that canyon
numen of secret gardens and hidden groves
who balanced the sunlight
on one palisaded wall
against the shadow on the other

whose voice was the little wind
playing among the oak leaves
or the strong wind of a storm
winding down the canyon as a warning
or the invitation of the canyon wren
or the dove's cooing

and will we see you again
as we drift on in darkness
followed by the moon's white face
floating on the surface of our lake
like the ghost of some dead thing

will we who never saw
you see your likes again
when we sink into the silk of earth
or when our ashes rock for a moment
on the surface of the water
perhaps the surface of a lake
of our own making before sliding down
will we know then at last
that we have always been blind
and will we see then what is gone
beyond all seeing

5
sink softly down
black silt to the canyon floor
as flower petals fall
as motes of sunlight drift through air
and settle in the evening
when the wind is still
sink softly down
fill the canyon from wall to wall
fall gently rain
upon the surface of this lake
shine softly moon and stars

it is no mirror for your light
it is the tomb of beauty
lost forever
and it is despair
the darkness in ourselves we fear

RICHARD SHELTON
(B. 1933)

You cannot convert the fragile stick nests of herons into timber or oil and gas; you cannot turn the whistle of wind across ancient orange sands into dollar bills or votes or security. You cannot cut a road into red rock, across a sand creek, and convert that loss into gain. This is and has always been a myth of mankind, of all countries both savage and civilized. There is a point reached in all cultures—a point of saturation—where each blade cut weakens a place, and the miracle of regeneration does not one day occur.

The explosive economic and cultural growth of the West occurs here and not in other places precisely because the land is still healthy. In such places as my home of Lincoln County, Montana, however, where the land has become unhealthy—where blade-cut saturation has not only been reached, but exceeded—now the communities and economies of both man and animal are unhealthy. The more timber we clearcut, the poorer we get; the more mines we dig, the poorer we get. The last of the money goes somewhere but never to us, and in the end we have nothing left—less than nothing.

Utah is the state by which I came into the West: the

place that as an artist was best for me. I learned to write and to look at the world in Texas and Mississippi—wonderful places for storytelling—but I wanted to find a land, a place, large enough to hold the feelings I held about the world, about this life we've been given. I wanted to explore what was possible, not just probable. I wanted more space in both the imagination and beneath my feet. And Utah's red wilderness and its forests had, and still have for me, the beautiful density of reality I was seeking: a density and grounding that in turn allowed my imagination to wander.

The unprotected wilderness of the West is one of our greatest strengths as a country. Another is our imagination, our tendency to think, rather than accept—to challenge, to ask why, and what if; to create, rather than to destroy. This questioning is a kind of wildness, a kind of strength, that many have said is peculiarly American.

Why is Congress placing that strength in jeopardy—in Utah, in Montana, in Idaho, and in all of the American West? To lose Utah's wilderness would be to strip westerners and all Americans of a raw and vital piece of our soul, our identity, and our ability to imagine.

As a nation we are facing a crisis of the imagination.

I have lived and camped throughout the diminishing West—the diminishing wild Americas—and report to you that we are in a deficit condition of both wilderness and imagination; that we've taken from the land far beyond its capacity to give.

If we were talking about inflation or interest rates, I believe most members of Congress and the government would do everything in their power to shut down this arc of loss we find ourselves in. We all know that what is rare is always valuable, and wilderness is our rarest and most imperiled resource of all.

To hold on to one of the last things truly American and truly unique—a sense of place in the American West— would be an act of strength and a continued source of great power: not the West of the Marlboro Man and Chevrolet commercials, but the creative, healthy, and untouched West: the sage and pinyon, the rock and sand, the small burrowing owls, the herons. The glitter of stars on a clear small pool of water.

The print of a deer or lion in the sand, in untouched country, as you sleep—it is these things that allow you, allow us, to continue being American, rather than something-else, anything-else, everything-else.

RICK BASS
(B. 1958)

One morning at my riverside camp in Utah's Desolation Canyon I awoke to a glorious surprise. From river's edge to my open-air bed ran a swath of tracks and drip marks. The tracks curved around my sleeping bag in an easy lope then disappeared into the trees. The pale sand was pebbled with the drips of an unshaken pelt. The deepest paw prints were still dark brown and wet. Near my bed the creature grazed my toes. Mere inches closer it would have leapt over my head, and I would have stared up at the belly of a cougar.

The cougar brushed by me on one of hundreds of nights in Desolation Canyon, where I have lived and worked with my river-ranger husband for six years. Desolation is one of many wilderness study areas that could join a legacy of wild country like no other on the planet.

The Utah delegation's wilderness bill falls miserably short of this opportunity. It fails to include millions of acres of extraordinary land, and in an unprecedented biological sterilization of public policy, it prohibits agencies from protecting their natural values. The remnants of proposed wilderness are worm-holed with exemptions to roads, dams, and utility lines. Contrary to myth, the current law "locks out" machines, not people. This bill, in places, would lift the ban on the infernal combustion engine, as if the amputation of our vehicles from our persons on a mere fraction of public lands would cause undue suffering, not welcome relief from the techno-shriek of daily life. There is little "wild" in this wildlands bill; it erodes the idea of wilderness upon which we agreed as a country in 1964.

In this redrock desert, change is measured by sand drawn down the face and veins of the continent, grain by grain, a pace that defies America's compulsion to reduce the particularity of a place. In Utah, we still have islands of visible, palpable uniqueness. Here you can taste and feel color; the sheer immensity of distance becomes intimate. This land is remote, prickly, painfully beautiful. Its innate scarcities have preserved it despite a culture that mines, dams, and grids the rest of creation. Do we so lack in material well-being that we cannot leave the last 10 percent of Utah in its wild state? A hundred years ago desert-lover John C. Van Dyke lamented the dismissal of aesthetics as a highest good, lifeblood as vital as food and love. He said of the prevailing ethos, "The main affair of life is to get the dollar, and if there is any money in cutting the throat of Beauty, why, by all means, cut her throat." Can we afford to live without beauty?

We need wild country. We are mammals, not gods. We ask you to be visionary mammals. Others want political expedience. The latter would have you toss Utah's finest asset to the profit geeks and still end up in debt. Well, we've already done this in the West for a century. You could listen to those with a frontier hangover so great, they still reject any notion of limits, or you can heed the enlightened consensus of ecological sanity and a hunger for wild places. The visionary says — awkwardly, because it thwarts western history: We cannot measure this land with numbers or dollars. It looks so very peculiar, like red bones. But we need this strangely wild country, for here we can explore and rest and listen in an agreed peace.

When I tell the story of the cougar, friends ask, Were you terrified? No, I was half asleep, sensing a liquid ghost at the edge of my slumber. Had I been fully awake I would have been filled not with fear but with ecstasy. In its graceful arc over me the cougar didn't need my notice, only my care.

ELLEN MELOY
(B. 1946)

Basin. Fault. Range. Basin. Fault. Range. A mile of relief between basin and range. Stillwater Range. Pleasant Valley. Tobin Range. Jersey Valley. Sonoma Range. Pumpernickel Valley. Shoshone Range. Reese River Valley. Pequop Mountains. Steptoe Valley. Ondographic rhythms of the Basin and Range. We are maybe forty miles off the interstate, in the Pleasant Valley basin, looking up at the Tobin Range. At the nine-thousand-foot level, there is a stratum of cloud against the shoulders of the mountains, hanging like a ring of Saturn. The summit of Mt. Tobin stands clear, above the cloud. When we crossed the range, we came through a ranch on the ridgeline where sheep were fenced around a running brook and bales of hay were bright green. Junipers in the mountains were thickly hung with berries, and the air was unadulterated gin. This country from afar is synopsized and dismissed as "desert" — the home of the coyote and the pocket mouse, the side-blotched lizard and the vagrant shrew, the MX rocket and the pallid bat. There are minks and river otters in the Basin and Range. There are deer and antelope, porcupines and cougars, pelicans, cormorants, and common loons. There are Bonaparte's gulls and marbled godwits, American coots and Virginia rails. Pheasants. Grouse. Sandhill cranes. Ferruginous hawks and flammulated owls. Snow geese. This terrain is not corrugated, like the folded Appalachians, like a tubal air mattress, like a rippled potato chip. This is not—in that compressive manner—a ridge-and-valley situation. Each range here is like a warship standing on its own, and the Great Basin is an ocean of loose sediment with these mountain ranges standing in it as if they were members of a fleet without precedent, assembled at Guam to assault Japan. Some of the ranges are forty miles long, others a hundred, a hundred and fifty. They point generally north. The basins that separate them—ten and fifteen miles wide—will run on for fifty, a hundred, two hundred and fifty miles with lone, daisy-petalled windmills standing over sage and wild rye. Animals tend to be content with their home ranges and not to venture out across the big dry valleys.

Supreme over all is silence. Discounting the cry of the occasional bird, the wailing of a pack of coyotes, silence—a great spatial silence—is pure in the Basin and Range. It is a soundless immensity with mountains in it. You stand, as we do now, and look up at a high mountain front and turn your head and look fifty miles down the valley, and there is utter silence. It is the silence of the winter forests of the Yukon, here carried high to the ridgelines of the ranges. As

43

the physicist Freeman Dyson has written in *Disturbing the Universe,*

> It is a soul-shattering silence. You hold your breath and hear absolutely nothing. No rustling of leaves in the wind, no rumbling of distant traffic, no chatter of birds or insects or children. You are alone with God in that silence. There in the white flat silence I began for the first time to feel a slight sense of shame for what we were proposing to do. Did we really intend to invade this silence with our trucks and bulldozers and after a few years leave it a radioactive junkyard?

JOHN MCPHEE
(B. 1931)

First we pollute the wilderness, then we pollute our minds with the belief that we've done the right thing. Then we pollute the wilderness more because we've lost our ability to see it. Soon the wilderness ceases to exist. In its place is a garbage dump—vast and purposeless—and we think how wonderful we are to have created a place that speaks so well for what we are.

MARK STRAND
(B. 1934)

We need a pause the like of which we've never had in Western civilization. We need to halt at watershed junctures, like this one involving the disposition of Utah's public lands, and ask not only what is fair, just and reasonable, but what is enduringly wise.

The durable wealth of "public lands" lies beyond private bounty. Our principal task should not be to create new wealth but to manage the wealth we already have and which, for a variety of reasons, we cannot perceive.

In theory, publicly owned lands are publicly managed lands. In practice, the managing public comprises two opposing forces that government must reconcile: those with a specific economic interest and those without. As politics changes in the United States, one or the other of these two factions construes itself more (or less) influential in shaping public land policy. Neither group, of course, is ever in an unassailable position of authority, but public land decisions show a clear pattern. Land of little or no perceived economic utility tends to get protected; land showing any potential for economic profit—because it may support grass or timber or may harbor minerals or water—is contested. (It is also true in an economy like ours that the imperative to develop inevitably forces a subdivision of the public land under consideration, thus ensuring that at least some land is always released for development.)

We need a pause in Western society because the decision to develop a stretch of public land can't be reconsidered, and at present, we're making these irrevocable decisions in preemptive, fearful haste. Nearly anyone who has attended a public land hearing, in which opposing sides square off over economic issues and what are quite accurately called spiritual issues, is appalled by the rudeness and contempt that often characterize testimony. A disinterested observer feels saddened and embarrassed by the witless rhetoric, the false airs and vituperative retorts, the blind allegiance of some individuals in government, in the environmental movement, in industry. Citizens who speak from their hearts instead of their wallets are too often dismissed by hearing committees as "irrational."

We are not, of course, in dire need of roads, transmission towers, dams, reservoirs, and gas pipelines. We are in dire need of courtesy. We are in dire need of a broadly intelligent conversation about human fate. We are in need of a thorough and piercing review of our plan for human economic development, a plan that at best is a hugely expensive speculation about human needs.

We are not debating "wilderness" here in trying to decide the fate of Utah's undeveloped public lands. The term is too restrictive. We're debating the future direction of Western civilization, and our issue could not be more serious. A brutal, pointed lesson of human history is that unhealthy civilizations die. Civilizations that are physically, spiritually, or economically corrosive fall apart. Their people wither. If we do not want to pass away as a civilization, let alone as a Western nation, we need to recast our discussion so that it is this, not "wilderness," that is at stake. We need to see what a grave decision the release of public land for development is. If our central concerns remain who "wins" in these disagreements, or what sorts of "concessions" will please the most people, twenty years from now we'll be looked upon as fools. In a moment that called for discerning intelligence, we will be seen as people who settled for a fight over control, a venal and pedestrian aspiration.

The wisest thing now, it seems to me, is to regard undeveloped lands as an asset and to protect every acre of land possible. American culture, more than any other in the world, has been shaped by the image of private exploration of public land. The opportunity to still have that experience is deeply important to our sense of hope. And what you might call the principal, what's left in the account, is down to a pittance.

If we do not take the time now to understand where the diminishment of wilderness in America is taking us, the day will soon arrive when it will not matter. We will have given up a vision of heaven to bet we're not embarked on a trip to hell. The United States is a nation of staggering wealth. We can easily afford to conserve what we've been given and to wait patiently for a wisdom that so far has eluded us, a wisdom that will enable us to convey this gift, not simply consume it.

BARRY LOPEZ
(B. 1945)

There is a woman who is a tailor. She lives in Green River, Utah, and makes her livelihood performing alterations, taking a few inches here, letting out a few inches there, basting in hems then finishing them with a feather stitch.

While hiking in the San Rafael Swell, this woman was raped, thrown down face first on the sand. She never saw the face of her assailant. What she knew was this, that in that act of violence she lost her voice. She was unable to cry for help. He left her violated and raw.

The woman returned home and told no one of her experience. Instead, she grabbed a large spool of red thread, a pair of scissors and returned to the Swell.

The woman cut pieces of thread and placed them delicately on the desert. Six inches. Three inches. Twelve inches. They appeared as a loose stitched seam upon the land. She saw them as bloodlines, remembering the fetishes of Zuni she had held that draw the heart down. She recalled rabbit, lizard, and rattlesnake. She continued to cut lines in memory of animals she had known, seen, and spent time with in these redrock canyons: deer, mountain lion, flicker, and raven. And on one occasion, she recalled watching a black bear amble down Crack Canyon. For this creature, she left a line of red thread three feet long. She cut one-inch threads for frogs and left them inside potholes to wriggle in the rain when the basins would inevitably fill.

Time and space shift; it is fall. The woman is now walking along the banks of the Colorado River. She takes her spool of red thread, ties one end to a juniper and then begins walking with the river, following each bend, each curve, her red thread trailing behind her for miles, stitching together what she has lost.

It is spring. The woman is standing in the deep heat of the desert beside a large boulder known by locals as "the birthing rock." Tiny feet the size of her index finger are etched on stone. Ten toes of hope point to figures of women bearing down, legs spread, with the heads of children coming forth. She recognizes them as two beings seen as one, repeatedly.

The woman picks up an obsidian chip that has been worked by ancient hands, the flaked edge is razor sharp. She holds it between her fingers like a pencil, opens her left hand and traces her own lifeline from beginning to end. The crescent moon below her thumb turns red. She places her palm on the boulder and screams.

In the midst of the politics before us, I think of the woman in the San Rafael Swell and her spool of red thread basting memories back into the land.

Emily Dickinson writes, "Life is a spell so exquisite that everything conspires to break it."

How can we not respond?

Terry Tempest Williams

TERRY TEMPEST WILLIAMS
(B. 1955)

My son, Seth, had just arrived back from college, buoyant—ebullient—over finishing his sophomore year. His school was in the East, and he had told me that he wanted to celebrate his return by immersing himself in the West, the deepest and truest part of it we could find. We decided on the Canyon Country. The day after his plane landed in Denver, we headed out for hot, dry southern Utah.

One long hike took us down into a narrow canyon branching off the Escalante River. The sandstone walls, smoldering red, thrust straight up. Scattered pinyon and juniper, and ferns and grasses around the springs, accented the color embedded in the canyon sides.

This Wingate Sandstone had been the rock of surrounding mountain ranges. During the Triassic, some 200 million years ago, water worked the mountains, wearing them into sand. Winds lifted the grains and piled them up as dunes on the desert floor. The sands hardened back into rock. Then the whole Colorado Plateau rose, beginning just recently, perhaps 7 million years ago. The creek in this now-canyon would have none of it, resolutely holding its ground against the upthrusting Wingate and younger formations on top of it, cutting down 1,000 feet into rock and time. Much of the day we walked up to our calves in the creek.

In a rare wide spot in the canyon, behind a cluster of junipers, we found a panel of pictographs on the Wingate. The artisan painted this row of red and white images—supernatural and life-size—two thousand years ago, perhaps more. The three stolid figures had wide shoulders, narrow waists. We could see straight through the round staring eyes, and the eyes could see through us. We called it "Dream Panel."

Nearing dusk, we found the rock cairns marking the faint trail up and out. I've never done serious rock climbing, but Seth has. He instructed me on this climb, short of technical but still challenging. "Hug the slickrock with your body," he told me. "Always keep three firm holds. Take your time, Dad."

Halfway up, slightly shaken, still worrying about a fall, I told him, "You've got the right idea, Seth—I'll keep *four* firm holds."

Not long ago we scorned this land as remote, desolate. That thinking led to the post-war Big Buildup and the coal plants, dams, and uranium mines.

But today we know southern Utah, in the heart of the Colorado Plateau, for what it really is. The geologic events were so cataclysmic and so recent, and the frail soils so erodible, that the Colorado Plateau holds more graphic displays of exposed formation than anywhere on Earth. The dry air has preserved the ancient people's durable and magical rock art, villages, kivas, pots, and baskets to a degree found nowhere else.

Yet our society still seems to lack the will to care for the Canyon Country. The Utah congressional delegation—refusing to listen to the people, the canyons, or the old artisans—wants to declare some fragments of backcountry wilderness and then throw all the rest open to development.

That would be so shortsighted, so contemptuous of time. The old images on the walls were made so long ago, the walls themselves even longer. Time runs out to the future, too: give our grandchildren, and those far down the line from them, the blessing of taking a daughter or son into the weaving, rosy side canyons, of finding their own Dream Panels, and of being instructed by the young person on how to scramble out.

Time, oh, time.... May we not forsake you now.

CHARLES WILKINSON
(B. 1941)

For Gretchen
In our common love
of the Redrock country —

55

We praise our cities, our factories, mines, high-rise towers, all the structures that house our economic activities and satisfy our physical needs. We marvel at man's skill and ingenuity.

But when we need rest from our labor and release from the stress that civilization imposes, we don't look at skyscrapers. We leave the man-made creations, we leave the freeways and go where the natural world has not yet been destroyed. We go, if we are lucky and can afford it, to unmarked deserts, uncut forests, unpolluted shores. We breathe air with no stench of traffic fumes. We see animals that should remind us that we are not the only creatures that inhabit the earth. We return home refreshed and strengthened.

On the Pacific coast there is an area that progress, called development, is rapidly destroying. Each year condominiums creep higher up the foothills, like a vast institution for the psychically impaired. Bulldozers eat the remaining fields. What was once green and growing is concrete and asphalt. This fact is a warning for Utah, which is now threatened by exploitation and greed, and by shortsighted ignorance of what man needs to survive.

I sometimes vacation in a small canyon near this coastal land that exploitation is ruining. I feel threatened by the juggernaut of the future.

But sometimes at night, waking from dreams of being smashed or asphyxiated by machines, I hear in the blessed stillness of the little canyon the call of *Bubo,* the great horned owl. It is a dark and soothing sound, a lullaby for the world's woes, and my own. Somehow, he is surviving, though his fields diminish. His nonhuman voice restores my hope that the world is not quite lost.

OLIVE GHISELIN
(B. 1907)

The intent of this communication is to expose some dire consequences of supporting two proposals that have been introduced in Congress: HR 1745 in the House, S 884 in the Senate. I call for opposition. Enactment of those proposals would entail extensive and permanent damage to many of the richest wild lands of our inheritance and, in doing so, would deprive and impoverish us forever.

For the proposals in question comprise concessions permitting commercial enterprise to consume a body of irreplaceable resources, in a way and to an extent that would so deface vast reaches of the landscape that it could never recover.

Heedless self-service, greed, or shortage of understanding may lead individuals to ignore or reject such considerations. Lawmakers who concede approval invite reappraisal of their motives and of their fitness for leadership. To evade that conclusion should be impossible for dispassionate judgment.

Instead of further exposition or argument, I offer a perspective disentrammeled of factional pressures; a prospect illuminating present and future, envisaged from the high

summit of an undespoiled headland, above the Gulf of
Mexico, Sea of Cortés:

VANTAGE

I

All over the blue
Ocean the trees of the whales' breath:
All over the ocean,
Around the steeps of the headland
Falling westward and northward,
Punta Banda, and southward toward the turn of the land,
   three hundred miles,
Toward the lagoons, the pools of calm on the coast of
   deserts:
The fountains of the breath of the beasts
Whitening and leaning in the wind
On the ocean curve of the world,
Floating and misting,
Into mist

           into distance

                      into light.

The time is not yet
Of the continent-cities
And the forests cut.

When our age of glass is no more
Than glitter in dunes
Of detritus
The clouds will be here
In season, the water
Always.

The regret will be gone.

II
Ocean and air will lift
Shoring combers pluming
Over their leaning green
In landwind wings of spume.

If creatures astir on the cliffs
Have then the gift of light, let it
Be larger than ours, that lost
The world and took the moon.

BREWSTER GHISELIN
(B. 1903)

The clamshell opening of the cave sits a couple of hundred feet above the floor of the Great Basin Desert, where once the waters of the Great Salt Lake sparkled and flickered, where once a prehistoric people made a living and shared in the bounty of a wetter climate. This cave was not a permanent residence but a temporary one, utilized by archaic peoples on their never-ending rounds of hunting and gathering and fishing. I sit cross-legged, gazing out upon a vast landscape, reflecting on a lifestyle so different from mine.

During good growing years, when Indian populations were small, archaic life was good, for there was enough to eat. When times were bad and populations high, resources sparser and harder to find, life became poor to desperate. But out of these periods of stress came innovation, invention, and change. I, twentieth-century woman, rest here, settled in the silt of centuries, rolling the toothpick thigh bone of a mouse in my fingers, find this thought incredibly reassuring and ponder what I have come to understand about people who tracked these threadbare desert lands and my own necessity for clear horizons and long vistas.

Out here there is an order, a cause and effect that is logical and persistent. The sun always rises in the east.

Insights into this beautifully attuned world to which I am not adapted make the fine-tuning of those small creatures that hop and stalk, scurry and slither in the deserts objects of respect from which humans can extract survival skills and medical miracles: a kangaroo rat and a black-throated sparrow that survive well without free water; specialized toads that dream away the cold times burrowed far underground, metabolism slowed almost to zero; cactus wrens that preadjust their clutch size to the soon-to-be-available food. I tally the physiological adjustments of blood and urine, hearing and seeing, of adaptations in behavior that make life in the desert not only possible but possible with verve, qualities seen and unseen that spell not only survival, but survival with zest. I contemplate plants that can withstand salt-laden soils and those that cannot and their different modes of photosynthesis. I number the ingenious seeds that germinate under precise regimes and their measured sequences: time to remain dormant, time to sprout, time to flower and set seed, time to dazzle the desert. Utah's Great Basin Desert brims with good health and good spirits and a vibrating heat that locks in the marrow against a cold and lightless winter.

Scanning this irreplaceable desert below me, which has exacted its own tributes of this slow-boned human, memories come crowding to my mind of the gifts these desert years have laid on my doorstep, a mosaic of experiences made up of sprigs of creosote bush and sagebrush, an owl feather and a grasshopper wing, and a chip of obsidian tied up with the song of a spadefoot toad, my own medicine bundle for my own ceremonies of passage. The desert grants each of us our own understandings, charges us with the preservation of its messages.

To the west a single thin cloud hangs over the evening mountains, a vasa murrhina cloud illuminated from beneath. Alone in the sky, it incandesces as I watch, then fades. The ends still glow while the middle darkens to absorb the mountains beneath.

The sky behind the mountains segues to a pale steely blue, without warmth, bending upward to dusk. Where the sun has departed, the sky bleaches. Dust spirits sleep. A Cyclops moon rises to the east. The wind abides. Silence streams from the mountains. Black feathers of darkness drift downward, and the desert comes alive.

ANN ZWINGER
(B. 1925)

What is it that awakens in my soul when I walk in the desert, when I catch the scent of rain, when I see the sun and moon rise and set on all the colors of the earth, when I approach the heart of wilderness? What is it that stirs within me when I enter upon sacred ground? For indeed something does move and enliven me in my spirit, something that defines my very being in the world. I realize my humanity in proportion as I perceive my reflection in the landscape that enfolds me. It has always been so. The equation of man and earth is ancient and sacred. It is the cornerstone of religion; it is the great metaphor of belief, of wonder and holy regard, of profound reverence and deepest delight.

As my eyes search the prairie

I feel the summer in the spring.

That is to say, I am alive. I feel the pulse of the living earth. My being extends to all horizons; I am one with creation; I have a rightful place in the infinite design of the universe. I drift easily in the current of my life and in the current of all life. For the earth is alive and possessed of spirit. To know this is the proof of my belonging. My existence is appropriate to the earth and sky, the sun and moon. To no season am I a stranger, to no animal or tree. I am at home in the world.

N. SCOTT MOMADAY
(B. 1934)

What if every decision-maker were to admit that places can influence our destinies as much as other people can? What if each of us took it upon ourselves to honor and care for places luminous in our childhood or teenage memories much the way some of us have attempted to honor and care for revered elders?

If each of us acknowledges our indebtedness to such places of the heart—those which have shaped who we have become or who we wish to be—then we must figure out a practical way to "acknowledge this national debt" or, better, to invest in those places that nurture the American spirit.

The redrock canyon country of southern Utah was the first unimaginably large wilderness I ever encountered. My experience there just prior to my eighteenth birthday, plain and simple, initiated me into manhood. I owe much of who I am today to that timely exposure to pinyons and junipers more ancient than European settlement of this continent and to those sheer walls of Navajo Sandstone more immense than anything I had ever seen made by human hands. I was struck dumb by the ways in which its prehistoric granaries and petroglyphs spoke to me about how elegantly humans can adapt to a terrain dominated by slickrock and riddled with hidden gardens, living admirably within its constraints. Two decades later, I met a woman who grew up in what was then Arches National Monument, a woman who has become my wife; her childhood there ensured that she would always have canyon sand in her soul.

The Colorado Plateau opened up possibilities for our lives that no other country could have offered. It was there that I first heard these spare words from St. Francis of Assisi: "All which you used to avoid will bring you great sweetness and exceeding joy." Most of us have spent ample time with humans, but all too often, we have avoided immersing ourselves in the other-than-human world. And now a patch of the world still largely untrammeled by humans—the collective significance of various proposed wilderness areas of southern Utah—is gravely imperiled.

We must now try to fathom whether or not we will be leaving more of that wilderness protected or more of it destroyed by the time we die. What wild terrain will future generations have to inspire them as a natural benchmark by which to measure cultural and ecological health? Already, a larger proportion of children than ever before in human history grow up without access to wild places, wild plants, and wild animals. Failure to protect remaining sizable tracts of wilderness is tantamount to robbing future generations of their chance to be fully engaged with such wildness, the matrix within which our minds, hearts, and spirits evolved. To live in a world devoid of any wilderness of the likes of that lying within slickrock country is to be less than fully human. We must decide now whether we want to allow our generation to bear responsibility for impoverishing the world to a greater extent than any other generation on Earth has ever done. How dear to us is this redrock place in our hearts?

GARY PAUL NABHAN
(B. 1952)

The sun fell and left us with a long time to see the hills along the Big Blackfoot River as simply a dark and undulating subtext beneath a sky that was both spectacular and unsettling, close to frightening. We are nothing if not mystified amid glories.

Islands of cloud were silver to orange and occasional red. The pale sky beyond was perfect with infinities. In that moment I felt grief for the passing of our lives and recognized the possibility that we might come to find solace in the simple notion that we have no choice but to be part of such energies.

This last spring, in twilight across the upper meadow, thirty-seven thick-bodied elk were playing, limber and quick as they forgot their grazing and danced around chasing one another.

Annick and I stood in the strawberry garden, watching as a young mule came cantering toward them, trying to herd them or join them. The elk raised their heads and spooked away into the fringes of old-growth forest. They turned smokey in the twilight and then they were gone.

The young mule was left prancing there, alone like us.

We have no choice but to understand ourselves and the movements of our lives in the run of evolving energies that is nature. The animal we are evolved in such connections, the need is built in to our genetic makeup. Without intimacy, with one another and with nature, we tend to slide off into insanities.

We have nowhere to live except in nature. Ruin that which is natural and we will soon lose entire track of ourselves. Lose contact with that which is wild and we fall out of touch with all that this animal we are is able to understand as actual.

We go dizzy trying to live inside a virtual, make-believe world (like cities in space). As individuals and as a society, when we are out of touch with that which is natural, we go literally insane. We see such craziness each day, reported in every newspaper we read.

The only story we really know how to inhabit is the ancient one about ourselves in the natural world. As the setting for that story vanishes we begin to lose contact with our animal selves and become increasingly disoriented, disenfranchised.

Some of us are driven frantic and ultimately savaged by our anxieties. We don't know who we are; we don't know who we should want to be. Some of us begin to become monstrous.

If we hope to live in sane ways, we have no choice but to cherish and sustain those parts of the world that remain at least partways natural and intact. Without wilderness we start turning into not much of anybody; we lose track of our natural goodness, our capacity for compassion and empathy; we wander off in pursuit of unnatural desires. All cruelties are possible.

Like that young mule, we are alone, prancing around and out of love, impoverished, desperate in our isolations, driven to insanities of self-preoccupation and greed, literal indecencies. As we destroy that which is natural we eat ourselves alive.

WILLIAM KITTREDGE
(B. 1932)

When I drive to my mother's from my home in western Montana, I take a trip through loss and gain. Along the way, I think a lot, and sometimes think out loud. I wish that somehow each of you could sit with me as I drive and think and talk, for I believe that if you could hear what passes through my heart and mind as I cross the magnificence between my home and my mother's, surely you would pass the bill we call "America's Redrock Wilderness Act."

We'd drive the back roads down to Utah, you and I together, to see my eighty-year-old mother in the little Mormon village of Orangeville. Leaving Montana, we'd suddenly cross into the part of Idaho where everything claims to be lost but we would feel found. We'd drop over Lost Trail Pass into Salmon, which is now almost a lost fish, and head up the Lemhi Valley along the Lost River Range, and pretty soon we'd be cruising along the Lost River itself, down to the place known as the Sinks where the river really does get lost, vanishes in a long wallow of wet sand, into the caves and whorls of the broken basalt where it must follow its own pathways like the ways the blood gets back to the heart.

A little ways past the Idaho-Utah border, the real losses begin, and we would behold those, too, and marvel. They are the losses that come with our two centuries of American restlessness, the increasing, unceasing velocity with which we live our lives and make our livings. These are the losses that occur when we supplant everything else's habitat with our own. They are, in part, the losses reaped by our liberty, and as we talk and drive, I would impress upon you that for me, too, that liberty is every bit as precious as the wilderness I love. In fact, as I would tell you, I don't think you can tear the two apart without losing both, for our American liberty and our American wilderness have always been intertwined.

The losses we would feel together begin at Tremonton near the Idaho border and stretch all the way to Spanish Fork south of Provo. It's an eighty-mile-long, thirty-mile-wide megalopolis now, a place, yes, of freedoms and dreams, of commerce and industry and jobs, of the chaotic rumble of human creativity and the strange orderliness wrought by the invisible hand. And it is at once beautiful and terrible — the robust cacophony of economic freedom; just another bland strip of anyplace slipping precariously toward no place. Where from my childhood I remember endless orchards near Brigham City and Fruitvale, we would now see endless subdivisions, parking lots, business parks, malls. Up the face of the Wasatch Range, we'd see the miniature forests of Gambel oaks torn to shreds by bulldozers to make room for the swelling sea of humanity. Down in the low swales in the catchment of the Great Salt Lake, we would find our eyes searching hopefully for places that can't be developed. We'd peer into salty sloughs and willow-choked creek bottoms between those five-hundred-unit "planned" subdivisions and thrill to see the ibises and curlews and avocets down there, making their livings the way they have for millennia. Amid the crush of the world we have made, how much time do they have left?

A half-day later, we'd stand at the edge of the San Rafael Swell, where my life began. On the southern rim of what we can see from my mother's yard soars a skyline like nothing else on earth. It's the gateway to Canyon Country, a towering, upthrust edge of sandstone so torn and red it looks like a wound in the earth. From the time I can first remember it at age six until today, it quickens my imagination like no place else. The Head of Sinbad. Swazy's Leap. Black Dragon Canyon. Buckhorn Flat. The Devil's Racetrack. Carry water and use your wits.

As we stare across that massive invagination, that expanse of sixty miles we can see across the San Rafael, I would try to convince you that wilderness and liberty do not cancel each other out, but are symbiotic—indeed, are the oldest, most deeply ingrained elements of the American experiment.

I would know that you have heard it all before, because I have too. Writers, scientists, scholars, philosophers far more sophisticated than I have extolled, will continue to extol, the virtues of wilderness as a reservoir of genetic diversity, as the storehouse for future medical discoveries, as the source material of our human souls, as the control plots against which we can measure the ravages of Progress, as God's (or Gaia's) ancient cathedral, as the last of the least and the best of the rest. I try to avoid arguments with those more sophisticated than myself, but as I would explain to you there in my mother's yard, I think all of our "reasons" for preserving wilderness are quite beside the point.

We want to keep our American wilds, quite simply, because we are among the last industrial people who have had sustained contact with the kind of land we now call wilderness; it has been among us and within us, sometimes dominating our puny attempts at civilization, for as long as we have agreed to make a nation together. Love it, hate it, or ignore it, wilderness is in our American soul, and we are loath to give it up, or see it become so diminished, so vestigial, that it ceases to be what it has always been to us — those cussed, godforsaken, dangerous patches of outback full of things that can kill us. Carry water and use your wits.

The Utah wilderness is really all that's left of that place I knew as a child — that land so exotic, so holy, that many of its natives still refer to it as Zion. My home state is blessed with a federal law, the Wilderness Act of 1964, that allows the preservation of its backcountry in something resembling its original state, the smoldering red state in which God left it after Creation. All Utahns have to do is invoke that powerful law, that island of poetry in a sea of prosaic statutes, to preserve a little of what little is left. That Utahns seem reluctant to do so means that they need help, for those parts of Utah that qualify for inclusion among the designated wilderness lands do not belong only to Utah. They belong to all of us and, ultimately, to humanity. That these last few wild lands are rare and getting rarer has been said a million times. What has not been said nearly so much is this: these lands in their original state have everything to do with our character; lose them, and we are no longer the people we have always been.

DONALD SNOW
(B.1951)

I think we in Utah stand at a genuine fork in the road. Defining moments really do happen, and this is one. What we choose to do about the wilderness will reveal precisely who we think we are and what we think this life is all about. And our decision will color the quality of life in our state for — possibly — centuries to come.

One road leads to full protection of the BLM wilderness in the state, 5.7 million acres, which would amount to about 10 percent of Utah — a tithe. Now what is a tithe, psychologically and morally speaking? A giver of a tithe says: there is something greater than me and my needs and desires. There is something that gives me life and gives that life meaning. I willingly forego that 10 percent, in true recognition of my fortune, in true gratitude to the world. I trust.

Some of us tithe to human institutions. Behind all institutions, behind all humanity, giving them the breath they breathe before they even start to talk about themselves, stands wild nature. The universe is wild. We did not make it. Are we ready to recognize the gift of life?

Down the other road before us is a grudging, partial tithe — about one-third of a real tithe. Down this road, we give only what we didn't want anyway. This is the road of lip service to the wild earth, of paltry, niggling, so-called bottom-line-oriented thinking, of a selfishness so brazen it should be embarassingly obvious to all. As a Utahn for forty years, I am ashamed that my political representatives have chosen this road. Apparently they have not really recognized, spiritually, where they live. Our political representatives are wrong about the bottom line. The real bottom line is the diversity and health of the natural world, the world that grew us and in which, every breathing day, we have our being.

The wild gives Utah its distinctiveness and its identity and stands behind its quality of life. The battle over how much wilderness to protect is a true struggle for Utah's soul. I would like to believe we are aware enough, and grateful enough, to make a full tithe.

Tom Lyon

THOMAS J. LYON
(B. 1937)

There may be people who feel no need for nature. They are fortunate, perhaps. But for those of us who feel otherwise, who feel something is missing unless we can hike across land disturbed only by our footsteps or see creatures roaming freely as they have always done, we are sure there should be wilderness. Species other than man have rights too. Having finished all the requisites of our proud, materialistic civilization, our neon-lit society, does nature, which is the basis for our existence, have the right to live on? Do we have enough reverence for life to concede to wilderness this right?

Margaret E. Murie

MARGARET E. MURIE
(B. 1902)

Contributors

RICK BASS lives in northwest Montana's unprotected Yaak Valley. His short stories have appeared in *The Paris Review* and other magazines. His books include *In the Loyal Mountains, Winter, The Ninemile Wolves, Platte River, The Lost Grizzlies,* and others. *The Book of Yaak* will be published in October of 1996. He is also working on a novel, *Where the Sea Used to Be.*

BREWSTER GHISELIN is an artist and critic as well as a poet. His book *The Creative Process* has been in print for more than forty years and has won wide acclaim. His other books include *Country of the Minotaur, Light, Windrose: Poems 1929–1979,* and most recently, *Flame.* He has received the Blumenthal-Leviton-Blonder Prize, the Levinson Prize (of *Poetry*), and an award from the American Academy of Arts and Letters. He lives in Salt Lake City with his wife, Olive Ghiselin, where he is emeritus professor at the University of Utah.

OLIVE GHISELIN has been writing short stories for more than thirty years. Her books include *The Testimony of Mr. Bones,* winner of a 1990 Regional Book Award from the Mountains and Plains Booksellers Association, and *In Dust and Water.* She lives with her husband, Brewster Ghiselin, in Salt Lake City.

WILLIAM KITTREDGE grew up on and then managed his family's cattle ranch in the Great Basin, in southeast Oregon. He has taught in the English department at the University of Montana for twenty-five years and lives in Missoula. His books include the short story collections *The Van Gogh Field* and *We Are Not In This Together;* the essays, *Owning It All* and *Who Owns the West?;* and a memoir, *Hole In the Sky.* In a 1994 White House ceremony, President Clinton presented Kittredge with the Frankel Award for service to the humanities.

BARRY LOPEZ won the 1986 National Book Award in nonfiction for *Arctic Dreams.* His work gives equal weight to short stories (most recently, *Field Notes*) and to narratives about landscape and ideas. *Of Wolves and Men* won the John Burroughs Medal for natural history writing. His other books include *Crossing Open Ground, The Rediscovery of North America,* and *Crow and Weasel.* Lopez has received a Guggenheim fellowship, a Lannan Award, and an Award in Literature from the American Academy of Arts and Letters. He lives along the McKenzie River in Oregon.

THOMAS J. LYON teaches English at Utah State University in Logan, Utah, and is the editor of the quarterly journal *Western*

American Literature. He has also edited a number of anthologies, including *Great and Peculiar Beauty: A Utah Reader, A Literary History of the American West,* and *This Incomperable Lande: A Book of American Nature Writing.* He received the Governor's Award in the Humanities in 1995 from the Utah Humanities Council. His current writing includes *The Wildness That Is in Us: How and Why to Write about Nature.*

JOHN MCPHEE is a Ferris Professor of Journalism at Princeton University. He became a staff writer for *The New Yorker* in 1964, and his writing appears there before being released as books. McPhee's subject matter is extraordinarily diverse. His books include *Encounters with the Archdruid, Coming into the Country, Rising from the Plains,* and *Basin and Range* (Farrar, Straus & Giroux), from which his *Testimony* essay derives. His many awards include the Burroughs Medal for *The Control of Nature.*

ELLEN MELOY lives in Bluff, Utah. Her work with her husband as a river ranger in a remote canyon in southern Utah led to *Raven's Exile: A Season on the Green River,* winner of the Spur Award. Meloy's essays are widely anthologized, and she is a frequent commentator for National Public Radio for Utah. Her new work of nonfiction, *The Last Cheater's Waltz,* is in progress.

N. SCOTT MOMADAY won the Pulitzer Prize for *House Made of Dawn* in 1969. Novelist, poet, and painter, he grew up in the

Southwest, where his parents taught in reservation schools. His book *The Way to Rainy Mountain* traces the journey of his people, the Kiowa, from the Rocky Mountains to the Oklahoma plains. His other books include *The Names* and *The Ancient Child.* He has won the Premio Letterario Internazionale "Mondello" and now lives in Tucson, where he teaches at the University of Arizona as Regent's Professor of English.

MARGARET E. MURIE, "the first lady of conservation," has worked and written tirelessly on behalf of wilderness, particularly in the Arctic. Until his death in 1963, she and her husband, Olaus J. Murie, worked together as exemplified in their book *Wapiti Wilderness.* Her books include *Two in the Far North* and *Island Between.* Her many awards include the Robert Marshall Award given by The Wilderness Society, an organization virtually embodied by the Muries from the 1940s to the early 1960s. Mrs. Murie lives in Moose, Wyoming.

GARY PAUL NABHAN, ethnobotanist, teacher, and writer, lives in Tucson, Arizona, where he cofounded Native Seeds/SEARCH and works as director of science for the Arizona-Sonora Desert Museum. A MacArthur Fellow, Pew Scholar, and winner of the Premio Gaia, his books include *Gathering the Desert* (which won the Burroughs Medal), *The Desert Smells Like Rain,* and *The Geography of Childhood: Why Children Need Wild Places* (with Stephen Trimble). *Canyons of Color: Utah's Slickrock Wildlands,* coauthored with his wife, Caroline Wilson, who grew up in

Arches, highlights his twenty-five years of being humbled by Utah's slickrock.

RICHARD SHELTON is Regent's Professor of English at the University of Arizona. His book *Going Back to Bisbee* won the Western States Book Award. His many volumes of poetry include *Selected Poems, 1969–1982*. The Sierra Club commissioned "Glen Canyon on the Colorado." It premiered in Salt Lake City on the anniversary of the building of Glen Canyon Dam. Born in Idaho, Shelton lives in Tucson, Arizona.

KAREN SHEPHERD is a former member of Congress from Utah. She grew up near the areas now being proposed for wilderness and was a strong advocate for environmental issues while she was in office. She has been an English teacher, mazagine editor, publisher, columnist, university administrator, and fellow at Harvard's Institute of Politics. Her award-winning articles, addressing politics, the environment, women's issues, and management, span sixteen years.

DONALD SNOW was born in Price, Utah, and as a child lived in the nearby coal mining camp of Hiawatha, where his father worked as night shift foreman at the King Mine. He lives in Missoula, Montana, where he teaches in the University of Montana environmental studies program. He is founder and coeditor of the award-winning *Northern Lights* magazine and has recently launched a new triquarterly journal, *The Chronicle of*

Community. His books include *Northern Lights: A Selection of New Writing from the American West* (with Deborah Clow) and *The Next West: New Perspectives on Public Lands, Economics and Community in the American West* (with John Baden).

MARK STRAND was chosen Poet Laureate of the United States by the Librarian of Congress in 1990. His books include *Reasons for Moving, The Story of Our Lives, Selected Poems, The Continuous Life,* and *Dark Harbor.* For over ten years, he taught at the University of Utah. He now teaches at Johns Hopkins University. A MacArthur Fellow, he has also received fellowships from the Academy of American Poets and the Guggenheim and Rockefeller foundations.

STEPHEN TRIMBLE, writer and photographer, lives in Salt Lake City. He worked as a park ranger at Arches and Capitol Reef National Parks in the 1970s and, later, as director of the Museum of Northern Arizona Press. His books include *Blessed By Light: Visions of the Colorado Plateau, The People: Indians of the American Southwest, The Geography of Childhood: Why Children Need Wild Places* (with Gary Paul Nabhan), and *The Sagebrush Ocean: A Natural History of the Great Basin,* winner of the Ansel Adams and Earle Chiles awards. He won a Frank Waters Southwest Writing Award for a short story set in the southern Utah wilderness.

ANN WEILER WALKA is a poet and the former museum educator at the Museum of Northern Arizona. She is at home both in

Flagstaff, Arizona, and in southern Utah, where she naturalizes and writes and is building a house. Her first book, *Waterlines: Journeys on a Desert River*, is a collection of poems about the San Juan River. A fellowship from the Arizona Commission on the Arts partly funded her new manuscript, *The Unknown River*.

T. H. WATKINS is the editor of *Wilderness*, the magazine of The Wilderness Society. In addition to more than 250 articles and reviews, he is the author of 25 other books, including *Righteous Pilgrim: The Life and Times of Harold L. Ickes*, a finalist for the National Book Award, and winner of the 1991 *Los Angeles Times* award for biography. His recent book, *Stone Time*, is a meditation on Utah's Canyon Country.

CHARLES WILKINSON, the Moses Lasky Professor of Law at the University of Colorado, has written widely on history, law, and society in the American West. His most recent books are *The Eagle Bird* and *Crossing the Next Meridian: Land, Water, and the Future of the West*. A member of the Governing Council of The Wilderness Society, he is presently writing a book about the Colorado Plateau.

TERRY TEMPEST WILLIAMS is a Utah native and naturalist-in-residence at the Utah Museum of Natural History. She is the author of *Pieces of White Shell: A Journey to Navajoland, Coyote's Canyon, Refuge: An Unnatural History of Family* and *Place, An Unspoken Hunger*, and most recently, *Desert Quartet*. She has received a Lannan Literary Fellowship in creative nonfiction and currently serves on the board of the Southern Utah Wilderness Alliance. She was recently inducted into the Rachel Carson Institute's Honor Roll.

ANN ZWINGER is a recipient of the John Hay Medal of The Orion Society. Her books include *Run River Run,* about the Green River (winner of the Burroughs Medal); *Wind in the Rock,* a journey into Utah's proposed San Juan-Anasazi wilderness; and *Downcanyon: A Naturalist Explores the Colorado River through the Grand Canyon,* winner of the Western States Book Award. Artist and art historian by training and naturalist by inclination, she lives in Colorado Springs, Colorado, and is an adjunct professor at Colorado College.

Acknowledgments

Nothing exists in isolation. *Testimony* owes its momentum to the belief and expertise of the following individuals:

In Salt Lake City: Trent Alvey and Carl Trujillo, of Trent Alvey Design, and Alan Hills of West Wind Litho; former Congresswoman Karen Shepherd, for her wise counsel and insight into the political process; and Annette and Ian Cumming, for their generosity in funding the congressional edition of *Testimony.*

In Washington, D.C.: Mike Burke, for donating his time to arrange the press conference in Washington, D.C.; Diane MacEachern from Vanguard Communications, for her help in communicating these ideas to the press; Chris Arthur, legislative director for Rep. Maurice Hinchey; Kerri McClimen, press secretary for Rep. Bruce Vento; Mary Francis-Repko, legislative assistant to Senator Russell Feingold; and, of course, Congressmen Maurice Hinchey and Bruce Vento, along with Senator Russell Feingold, for their bold leadership. In March 1996, Senator Bill Bradley

(D-NJ) led the filibuster that, for now, has forced the Utah delegation to withdraw their radical bill; we thank him for his courage and for reading from *Testimony* on the Senate floor.

In the conservation community: Bob Bingaman, Lawson LeGate, and Rudy Lukez from The Sierra Club, along with Fran Hunt, Pam Eaton, Jerry Greenberg, and Mary Hanley at The Wilderness Society, joined with the staff of the Southern Utah Wilderness Alliance to distribute copies of *Testimony* throughout the conservation community. Liz McCoy of the Utah Wilderness Coalition has our gratitude and highest regard for organizing the grass roots across the country in wholehearted activism on behalf of America's Redrock Wilderness.

In particular, we wish to thank the entire staff of the Southern Utah Wilderness Alliance for their belief in the power of grassroots activism. Without their leadership and keen understanding of how we, as citizens, might engage in the political process, and without their good humor and savvy, we may not have dared to enter this unknown territory. Mike Matz, Ken Rait, Scott Groene, Heidi McIntosh, Tom Price, Amy O'Connor, Erin Moore, Dave Pachew, Kris Edwards, Amy Barry, Brant Calkin, and, especially, Cindy Shogan have our deepest respect and gratitude.

We appreciate the staff of Milkweed Editions: Gayle Peterson, for widening the circle of *Testimony* in fostering a

"Literature for a Land Ethic," and Beth Olson, for elegantly managing the editorial and production details.

And finally, we wish to thank Emilie Buchwald, publisher of Milkweed Editions, for understanding the spirit of this book so clearly, that this dialogue on behalf of all wildlands might continue.

Appendix

History of Testimony

Letter Sent to Contributors

On August 3, 1995, the following letter was sent to twenty-five writers whose souls are tied to the West.

Dear Friends:

Summer greetings. We need your help. The Utah Congressional delegation has placed a dreadful wilderness bill before Congress, calling for only 1.8 million acres of protected lands out of 22 million of BLM lands in Utah. In its details, this bill undermines the integrity of the 1964 Wilderness Act. HR 1745 (and its corresponding bill in the Senate, S 884) is unprecedented in its "hard release" language and provisions for gas pipelines, communication towers, and dams. It is another example of Congress' attack on the ecological health and well-being of this nation.

We cannot afford to be cynical. We can respond.

As writers tied to this place, we can speak to the fundamental values of the opposing position, of the critical need to support the Citizen's Proposal of 5.7 million acres, drafted over many years by the Utah Wilderness Coalition, now embodied in HR 1500, "America's Redrock Wilderness Act."

We write to ask you, along with the writers above, to donate a short piece for a chapbook we will design and bind with care and place on the desk of every congressperson and senator by the end of September. We are also working on a special congressional luncheon and press conference where these essays would be introduced. We ask for no more than three double-spaced pages— the most eloquent, most impassioned, most reasoned essay you have ever crafted in the name of wildness. We hope for words that match in spirit Wallace Stegner's "geography of hope" from "Wilderness Coda." We can write to unsettle, to move, to convince.

We believe these essays can make a difference by elevating the level of discussion to one of soulful contemplation on behalf of all lands in North America, their spiritual value, their psychological as well as biological necessity.

In order to deliver this collection to Congress by the end of September— before a vote— we need your piece by the end of August. We know this is short notice but we feel we can ask this of our community. If you have the time to contribute, please send your piece to Terry as Steve will be out of town from August 12–30. Feel free to call either of us with questions.

Thank you for your gifts of language and hard work.
For the land, for each other,

Stephen Trimble   Terry Tempest Williams

Letters Sent to Congress

In fall 1995, Representatives Bruce F. Vento and Maurice Hinchey and Senator Russell Feingold forwarded copies of the original edition of *Testimony* to members of the U. S. House and Senate. Representatives Vento and Hinchey sent the following letter on September 27.

Dear Colleague:

We have the good fortune to send along to you a rare item: not the usual Congressional testimony with its tedious prose replete with the obligatory statistics, charts and graphs, but rather a collection of essays and poems by some of America's most acclaimed living writers.

The attached "Chapbook" contains the works of Pulitzer Prize winner N. Scott Momaday; National Book Award winner Barry Lopez; best-selling author John McPhee; and former Poet Laureate of the United States Mark Strand. Indeed, twenty outstanding writers in all have contributed their eloquent and impassioned words about the need to preserve America's remaining wild lands, especially Utah's wilderness.

With just 1,000 of the books privately printed, Testimony *is both a powerful statement on behalf of wilderness and an extraordinarily rare literary work. From Tom Watkins' foreword to the compelling coda written by the amazing 93-year-old Margaret Murie, this book tells a convincing, moving story about the importance of wilderness to our American culture and the development of our unique American identity.*

Please read, enjoy, and contemplate this wonderful little book—and join us in support of the magnificent Utah Red Rock country that inspires these writers.

Senator Feingold sent the following letter to members of the U. S. Senate on October 12.

Dear Colleague:

Attached for your review is a copy of a recently released book containing essays and poems by 20 western naturalist writers reflecting their thoughts on Utah wilderness.

The book, entitled Testimony, *was released on September 27, 1995. It is modeled after the late Wallace Stegner's 1960 Wilderness Letter to the Kennedy Administration and was compiled during August 1995. The selections represent the opinions of the authors, and include writings by individuals such as Terry Tempest Williams, Utah native and author of five books; T. H. Watkins, editor of* Wilderness *magazine; N. Scott Momaday, winner of the 1969 Pulitzer Prize for* House Made of Dawn; *and Mark Strand, former Poet Laureate of the United States. 1,000 copies of this book have been printed. The writers donated their writings, and the printing costs were covered by a grant from the Cumming Foundation, which is based in Salt Lake City, Utah.*

As the Senate prepares to consider S 884, the Utah Public Lands Management Act, and other wilderness measures this Congress, this is an important book to review. I hope you will peruse this collection of writings for its creative merit, the effort it represents, and the insights it contains.

Utah Wilderness

Citizen Action Organizations

The citizen volunteers of the Utah Wilderness Coalition (led by Jim Catlin, Rod Greenough, Clive Kincaid, Mike Medberry, Fred Swanson, and Ray Wheeler) spent years developing a 5.7 million-acre wilderness proposal for the state. This proposal, detailed in the UWC book *Wilderness at the Edge* (1990), forms the basis of America's Redrock Wilderness Act, HR 1500, introduced in the last four congresses. Perhaps one day we will see this bill pass. All proceeds from the sale of *Testimony* will go to the Utah Wilderness Coalition, to fund grassroots organizing on behalf of Utah wilderness.

For further information, contact:
Utah Wilderness Coalition
P. O. Box 520974
Salt Lake City, UT 84152-0974

Southern Utah Wilderness Alliance
1471 South 1100 East
Salt Lake City, UT 84105-2423

Southern Utah Wilderness Alliance
215 Pennsylvania Ave. S. E., 3RD floor
Washington, DC 20003

Map of Utah Wilderness Areas

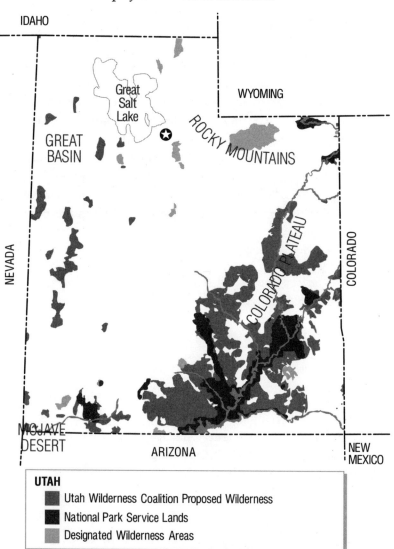

IDAHO

WYOMING

Great
Salt
Lake

GREAT
BASIN

ROCKY
MOUNTAINS

NEVADA

COLORADO PLATEAU

COLORADO

MOJAVE
DESERT

ARIZONA

NEW
MEXICO

UTAH
- Utah Wilderness Coalition Proposed Wilderness
- National Park Service Lands
- Designated Wilderness Areas

Proposed Wilderness Areas in Utah
[Area in acres, exlusive of State sections]

Area	UWC	BLM
Basin and Range Areas		
1. Little Goose Creek	1,300	0
2. Newfoundland Mts.	23,300	0
3. Silver Island Mtns.	27,200	0
4. Cedar Mtns.	62,100	0
5. Stansbury Mts.	22,500	10,480
6. Deep Creek Mts.	90,200	62,284
7. Fish Springs Range	55,200	33,840
8. Dugway Mts.	23,100	0
9. Rockwell	13,400	0
10. House Range	139, 400	77,176
11. Conger Mtn.	20,400	0
12. King Top	78,800	0
13. Wah Wah Mts.	109,700	36,382
14. Granite Peak	16,000	0
15. White Rock Range	3,900	3,820
16. Cougar Canyon-Docs Pass	29,400	4,228
Colorado Plateau Areas		
17. Beaver Dam Slopes	38,400	0
18. Red Mountain	18,500	12,842
19. Cottonwood Canyon	11,500	9,583
20. Greater Zion	132,775	61,540
21. Moqith Mountain	26,500	0
22. Upper Kanab Creek	42,200	0
23. Grand Staircase	268,300	100,142
24. Kaiparowits Plateau	650,500	91,361
25. Escalante Canyons	355,640	167,358
26. Henry Mountains	349,300	119,764
27. Dirty Devil	263,500	104,810
28. White Canyon	85,000	0
29. Glen Canyon	168,700	90,140
30. San Juan-Anasazi	395,800	204,090
31. Squaw and Cross Canyons	7,580	0
32. Dark Canyon	130,200	68,030
33. Canyonlands Basin	162,100	36,510
34. Behind the Rocks	51,100	12,635
35. La Sal Canyons	109,500	17,400
36. Westwater Canyon	37,600	31,200
37. Arches-Lost Spring Canyon	16,900	3,880
38. Labyrinth Canyon	171,700	56,500
39. San Rafael Swell	752,900	242,739
40. Book Cliffs-Desolation Canyon	718,600	327,955
41. White River	9,700	0
42. Greater Dinosaur	21,120	4,240
Total	*5,711,515*	*1,990,929*

Existing Designated Wilderness Areas in Utah

Area	Area in Acres
National Forest Areas (Designated 1979-84)	
A. Mt. Naomi	44,350
B. Wellsville Mtn.	23,850
C. High Uintas	460,000
D. Deseret Peak	25,500
E. Mt. Olympus	16,450
F. Twin Peaks	13,100
G. Lone Peak	30,088
H. Mt. Timpanogos	10,750
I. Mt. Nebo	28,000
J. Pine Valley Mountain	50,000
K. Ashdown Gorge	7,000
L. Box-Death Hollow	26,000
M. Dark-Woodenshoe Canyon	45,000
Total	*780,088*

BLM Areas (Designated in Arizona Wilderness Legislation in 1989)

Area	Area in Acres
N. Beaver Dam Mountains	2,597
O. Paria Canyon-Vermilion Cliffs	19,954
Total	*22,551*

The American Wilderness

List of United States Wilderness Areas

According to the Bureau of Land Management in Washington, D. C., the following areas were officially designated wilderness areas as of July 3, 1995. They are managed by the Bureau of Land Management (BLM), the Forest Service (FS), the Fish and Wildlife Service (FWS), and the National Park Service (NPS).

Wilderness Area Name (Federal only)	Size in Acres
Alabama	
Cheaha FS	7,245
Sipsey FS	25,906
Total Forest Service	
acres in Alabama:	*33,151*
State Total of Wilderness	
Acreage for Alabama:	*33,151*
Alaska	
Aleutian Islands FWS	1,300,000
Andreafsky FWS	1,300,000
Arctic FWS	8,000,000
Becharof FWS	400,000
Bering Sea FWS	81,340
Bogoslof FWS	175
Chamisso FWS	455
Chuck River FS	74,298
Coronation Island FS	19,232
Denali NPS	2,124,783
Endicott River FS	98,729
Forrester Island FWS	2,832
Gates of the Arctic NPS	7,167,192
Glacier Bay NPS	2,664,840
Hazy Island FWS	32
Innoko FWS	1,240,000
Izembek FWS	300,000
Karta River FS	39,889
Katmai NPS	3,384,358
Kenai FWS	1,350,000
Kobuk Valley NPS	174,545
Kootznoowoo FS	955,694
Koyukuk FWS	400,000
Kuiu FS	60,581
Lake Clark NPS	2,619,550
Maurelle Islands FS	4,937
Misty Fjords FS	2,142,243
Noatak NPS	5,765,427
Nunivak FWS	600,000
Petersburg Creek-Duncan Salt Chuck FS	46,77
Pleasant/Lemusurier/ Inian Islands FS	23,096
Russell Fjord FS	348,701
Saint Lazaria FWS	65
Selawik FWS	240,000
Semidi FWS	250,000
Simeonof FWS	25,855
South Baranof FS	319,568
South Etolin FS	83,371
South Prince of Wales FS	90,996
Stikine-LeConte FS	448,841
Tebenkof Bay FS	66,839
Togiak FWS	2,270,000

Tracy Arm-Fords Terror FS	653,179
Tuxedni FWS	5,566
Unimak FWS	910,000
Warren Island FS	11,181
West Chichagof-Yakobi FS	264,747
Wrangell-St. Elias NPS	9,078,675
Total Fish and Wildlife Service	
acres in Alaska:	*18,676,320*
Total National Park Service	
acres in Alaska:	*32,979,370*
Total Forest Service	
acres in Alaska:	*5,752,899*
State Total of Wilderness	
Acreage for Alaska:	*57,408,589*

Arizona

Apache Creek FS	5,666
Aravaipa Canyon BLM	19,700
Arrastra Mountain BLM	129,800
Aubrey Peak BLM	15,400
Baboquivari Peak BLM	2,040
Bear Wallow FS	11,080
Beaver Dam Mountains BLM	15,000
Big Horn Mountains BLM	21,000
Cabeza Prieta FWS	803,418
Castle Creek FS	25,215
Cedar Bench FS	14,950
Chiricahua FS	87,700
Chiricahua NPS	9,440
Cottonwood Point BLM	6,860
Coyote Mountains BLM	5,100
Dos Cabezas Mountains BLM	11,700
Eagletail Mountains BLM	100,600
East Cactus Plain BLM	14,630
Escudilla FS	5,200
Fishhooks BLM	10,500
Fossil Springs FS	22,149
Four Peaks FS	61,074
Galiuro FS	76,317
Gibraltar Mountain BLM	18,790
Grand Wash Cliffs BLM	37,030
Granite Mountain FS	9,762
Harcuvar Mountains BLM	25,050
Harquahala Mountains BLM	22,880
Hassayampa River Canyon BLM	12,300
Havasu FWS	14,606
Hells Canyon BLM	10,600
Hellsgate FS	37,440
Hummingbird Springs BLM	31,200
Imperial FWS	9,220
Juniper Mesa FS	7,406
Kachina Peaks FS	18,616
Kanab Creek FS	63,760
Kanab Creek BLM	6,700

Kendrick Mountain FS	6,510
Kofa FWS	516,200
Mazatzal FS	252,390
Miller Peak FS	20,190
Mount Baldy FS	7,079
Mount Logan BLM	14,650
Mount Nutt BLM	27,660
Mount Tipton BLM	32,760
Mount Trumbull BLM	7,880
Mount Wilson BLM	23,900
Mount Wrightson FS	25,260
Muggins Mountains BLM	7,640
Munds Mountain FS	24,411
Needle's Eye BLM	8,760
New Water Mountains BLM	24,600
North Maricopa Mountains BLM	63,200
North Santa Teresa BLM	5,800
Organ Pipe Cactus NPS	312,600
Paiute BLM	87,900
Pajarita FS	7,553
Paria Canyon-Vermilion Cliffs	
BLM	89,400
Peloncillo Mountains BLM	19,440
Petrified Forest NPS	50,260
Pine Mountain FS	20,061
Pusch Ridge FS	56,933
Rawhide Mountains BLM	38,470
Redfield Canyon BLM	9,930
Red Rock-Secret Mountain FS	47,194
Rincon Mountain FS	38,590
Saddle Mountain FS	40,539
Saguaro NPS	71,400
Salome FS	18,531
Salt River Canyon FS	32,101
Santa Teresa FS	26,780
Sierra Ancha FS	20,850
Sierra Estrella BLM	14,400
Signal Mountain BLM	13,350
South Maricopa Mountains BLM	60,100
Strawberry Crater FS	10,743
Superstition FS	159,757
Swansea BLM	16,400
Sycamore Canyon FS	55,937
Table Top BLM	34,400
Tres Alamos BLM	8,300
Trigo Mountains BLM	30,300
Upper Burro Creek BLM	27,440
Wabayuma Peak BLM	40,000
Warm Springs BLM	112,400
West Clear Creek FS	15,238
Wet Beaver FS	6,155
White Canyon BLM	5,790
Woodchute FS	5,833
Woolsey Peak BLM	64,000

Arkansas

California

Mecca Hills BLM	24,200
Mesquite BLM	47,330
Mojave NPS	695,200
Mokelumne FS	99,161
Monarch FS	44,896
Mount Shasta FS	33,845
Newberry Mountains BLM	22,900
Nopah Range BLM	110,860
North Algodones Dunes BLM	32,240
North Fork FS	7,999
North Mesquite Mountains BLM	25,540
Old Woman Mountains BLM	146,020
Orocopia Mountains BLM	40,735
Owens Peak BLM	74,060
Pahrump Valley BLM	74,800
Palen/McCoy BLM	270,629
Palo Verde Mountains BLM	32,310
Philip Burton NPS	25,370
Picacho Peak BLM	7,700
Pine Creek FS	13,480
Pinnacles NPS	12,952
Piper Mountain BLM	72,575
Piute Mountains BLM	36,840
Red Buttes FS	16,150
Resting Spring Range BLM	78,868
Rice Valley BLM	40,820
Riverside Mountains BLM	22,380
Rodman Mountains BLM	27,690
Russian FS	12,000
Sacatar Trail BLM	51,900
Saddle Peak Hills BLM	1,440
San Gabriel FS	36,118
San Gorgonio BLM	37,980
San Gorgonio FS	56,722
San Jacinto FS	32,248
San Mateo Canyon FS	38,484
San Rafael FS	197,380
Santa Lucia BLM	1,733
Santa Lucia FS	18,679
Santa Rosa BLM	64,340
Santa Rosa FS	13,787
Sawtooth Mounains BLM	35,080
Sequoia-Kings Canyon NPS	736,980
Sespe FS	219,700
Sheephole Valley BLM	174,800
Sheep Mountain FS	41,883
Silver Peak FS	14,500
Siskiyou FS	152,680
Snow Mountain FS	36,370
South Nopah Range BLM	16,780
South Sierra FS	60,084
South Warner FS	70,614
Stateline BLM	7,050
Stepladder Mountains BLM	81,600

Surprise Canyon BLM	29,180
Sylvania Mountains BLM	17,829
Thousand Lakes FS	16,335
Trilobite BLM	31,160
Trinity Alps BLM	4,623
Trinity Alps FS	498,141
Turtle Mountains BLM	144,500
Ventana FS	202,178
Whipple Mountains BLM	77,520
Yolla Bolly-Middle Eel BLM	7,145
Yolla Bolly-Middle Eel FS	146,696
Yosemite NPS	677,600
Total Fish and Wildlife Service	
acres in California:	*9,172*
Total Bureau of Land Management	
acres in California:	*3,587,395*
Total National Park Service	
acres in California:	*5,856,450*
Total Forest Service acres	
in California:	*4,398,919*
State Total of Wilderness	
Acreage for California:	*13,851,936*

Colorado

Black Canyon	
of the Gunnison NPS	11,180
Buffalo Peaks FS	43,410
Byers Peak FS	8,095
Cache La Poudre FS	9,238
Collegiate Peaks FS	166,716
Comanche Peak FS	66,791
Eagles Nest FS	132,906
Flat Tops FS	38,870
Flat Tops FS	196,165
Fossil Ridge FS	32,838
Great Sand Dunes NPS	33,450
Greenhorn Mountain FS	22,040
Holy Cross FS	122,388
Hunter-Fryingpan FS	82,729
Indian Peaks FS	70,374
Indian Peaks NPS	2,917
La Garita FS	129,629
Lizard Head FS	41,193
Lost Creek FS	119,790
Maroon Bells-Snowmass FS	180,962
Mesa Verde NPS	8,100
Mount Evans FS	74,401
Mount Massive FS	27,980
Mount Massive FWS	2,560
Mount Sneffels FS	16,565
Mount Zirkel FS	160,568
Neota FS	9,924
Never Summer FS	20,747
Platte River FS	743

Powderhorn BLM	48,115
Powderhorn FS	13,599
Ptarmigan Peak FS	13,175
Raggeds FS	64,928
Rawah FS	73,068
Sangre de Cristo FS	226,420
Sarvis Creek FS	47,140
South San Juan FS	158,790
Uncompahgre BLM	3,390
Uncompahgre FS	99,331
Vasquez Peak FS	12,300
Weminuche FS	487,704
West Elk FS	176,172
Total Fish and Wildlife Service	
acres in Colorado:	*2,560*
Total Bureau of Land Management	
acres in Colorado:	*51,505*
Total National Park Service	
acres in Colorado:	*55,647*
Total Forest Service	
acres in Colorado:	*3,147,686*
State Total of Wilderness	
Acreage for Colorado:	*3,257,398*

Florida

Alexander Springs FS	7,941
Big Gum Swamp FS	13,660
Billies Bay FS	3,092
Bradwell Bay FS	24,602
Cedar Keys FWS	379
Chassahowitzka FWS	23,580
Everglades NPS	1,296,500
Florida Keys FWS	6,197
Island Bay FWS	20
J.N. "Ding" Darling FWS	2,619
Juniper Prairie FS	14,277
Lake Woodruff FWS	1,066
Little Lake George FS	2,833
Mud Swamp/New River FS	8,090
Passage Key FWS	36
Pelican Island FWS	6
St. Marks FWS	17,350
Total Fish and Wildlife Service	
acres in Florida:	*51,253*
Total National Park Service	
acres in Florida:	*1,296,500*
Total Forest Service acres	
in Florida:	*74,495*
State Total of Wilderness	
Acreage for Florida:	*1,422,248*

Georgia

Big Frog FS	89
Blackbeard Island FWS	3,000
Blood Mountain FS	7,800
Brasstown FS	12,338
Cohutta FS	35,265
Cumberland Island NPS	8,840
Ellicott Rock FS	2,021
Mark Trail FS	16,400
Okefenokee FWS	353,981
Raven Cliffs FS	8,562
Rich Mountain FS	9,476
Southern Nantahala FS	11,770
Tray Mountain FS	9,702
Wolf Island FWS	5,126
Total Fish and Wildlife Service	
acres in Georgia:	*362,107*
Total National Park Service	
acres in Georgia:	*8,840*
Total Forest Service	
acres in Georgia:	*113,423*
State Total of Wilderness	
Acreage for Georgia:	*484,370*

Hawaii

Haleakala NPS	19,270
Hawaii Volcanoes NPS	123,100
Total National Park Service	
acres in Hawaii:	*142,370*
State Total of Wilderness	
Acreage for Hawaii:	*142,370*

Idaho

Craters of the Moon NPS	43,243
Frank Church-	
River of No Return FS	2,365,821
Frank Church-	
River of No Return BLM	802
Gospel Hump FS	205,764
Hells Canyon FS	83,811
Sawtooth FS	217,088
Selway-Bitterroot FS	1,089,017
Total Forest Service	
acres in Idaho:	*3,961,500*
Total National Park Service	
acres in Idaho:	*43,243*
Total Bureau of Land Management	
acres in Idaho:	*802*
State Total of Wilderness	
Acreage for Idaho:	*4,005,545*

Illinois

Bald Knob FS	5,863
Bay Creek FS	2,866
Burden Falls FS	3,671
Clear Springs FS	4,730
Crab Orchard FWS	4,050

Garden of the Gods FS	3,268
Lusk Creek FS	4,466
Panther Den FS	685
Total Fish and Wildlife Service	
acres in Illinois:	*4,050*
Total Forest Service	
acres in Illinois:	*25,549*
State Total of Wilderness	
Acreage for Illinois:	*29,599*

Indiana

Charles C. Deam FS	12,935
Total Forest Service	
acres in Indiana:	*12,935*
State Total of Wilderness	
Acreage for Indiana:	*12,935*

Kentucky

Beaver Creek FS	4,753
Clifty FS	11,662
Total Forest Service	
acres in Kentucky:	*16,415*
State Total of Wilderness	
Acreage for Kentucky:	*16,415*

Louisiana

Breton FWS	5,000
Kisatchie Hills FS	8,679
Lacassine FWS	3,346
Total Fish and Wildlife Service	
acres in Louisiana:	*8,346*
Total Forest Service	
acres in Louisiana:	*8,679*
State Total of Wilderness	
Acreage for Louisiana:	*17,025*

Maine

Baring Unit FWS	4,680
Birch Islands Unit FWS	6
Caribou-Speckled Mountain FS	12,000
Edmunds Unit FWS	2,706
Total Fish and Wildlife Service	
acres in Maine:	*7,392*
Total Forest Service	
acres in Maine:	*12,000*
State Total of Wilderness	
Acreage for Maine:	*19,392*

Massachusetts

Monomoy FWS	2,420
Total Fish and Wildlife Service	
acres in Massachusetts:	*2,420*
State Total of Wilderness	
Acreage for Massachusetts:	*2,420*

Michigan

Big Island Lake FS	5,856
Delirium FS	11,870
Horseshoe Bay FS	3,790
Huron Islands FWS	147
Isle Royale NPS	132,018
Mackinac FS	12,230
McCormick FS	16,850
Michigan Islands FWS	12
Nordhouse Dunes FS	3,450
Rock River Canyon FS	4,640
Round Island FS	378
Seney FWS	25,150
Sturgeon River Gorge FS	14,500
Sylvania FS	18,327
Total Fish and Wildlife Service	
acres in Michigan:	*25,309*
Total Forest Service	
acres in Michigan:	*91,891*
Total National Park Service	
acres in Michigan:	*132,018*
State Total of Wilderness	
Acreage for Michigan:	*249,218*

Minnesota

Agassiz FWS	4,000
Boundary Waters Canoe Area FS	807,451
Tamarac FWS	2,180
Total Fish and Wildlife Service	
acres in Minnesota:	*6,180*
Total Forest Service	
acres in Minnesota:	*807,451*
State Total of Wilderness	
Acreage for Minnesota:	*813,631*

Mississippi

Black Creek FS	5,052
Gulf Islands NPS	5,514
Leaf FS	994
Total National Park Service	
acres in Mississippi:	*5,514*
Total Forest Service	
acres in Mississippi:	*6,046*
State Total of Wilderness	
Acreage for Mississippi:	*11,560*

Missouri

Bell Mountain FS	8,977
Devils Backbone FS	6,595
Hercules-Glades FS	12,314
Irish FS	16,117
Mingo FWS	7,730
Paddy Creek FS	7,019
Piney Creek FS	8,087

Rockpile Mountain FS	4,089
Total Fish and Wildlife Service	
acres in Missouri:	*7,730*
Total Forest Service	
acres in Missouri:	*63,198*
State Total of Wilderness	
Acreage for Missouri:	*70,928*

Montana

Absaroka-Beartooth FS	920,327
Anaconda-Pintlar FS	158,014
Bob Marshall FS	1,009,356
Cabinet Mountains FS	94,272
Gates of the Mountains FS	28,562
Great Bear FS	286,700
Lee Metcalf-	
Bear Trap Canyon Unit BLM	6,000
Lee Metcalf FS	248,944
Medicine Lake FWS	11,366
Mission Mountains FS	73,877
Rattlesnake FS	32,844
Red Rock Lakes FWS	32,350
Scapegoat FS	239,296
Selway-Bitterroot FS	251,443
UL Bend FWS	20,819
Welcome Creek FS	28,135
Total Fish and Wildlife Service	
acres in Montana:	*64,535*
Total Bureau of Land Management	
acres in Montana:	*6,000*
Total Forest Service	
acres in Montana:	*3,371,770*
State Total of Wilderness	
Acreage for Montana:	*3,442,305*

Nebraska

Fort Niobrara FWS	4,635
Soldier Creek FS	7,794
Total Fish and Wildlife Service	
acres in Nebraska:	*4,635*
Total Forest Service	
acres in Nebraska:	*7,794*
State Total of Wilderness	
Acreage for Nebraska:	*12,429*

Nevada

Alta Toquima FS	38,000
Arc Dome BLM	20
Arc Dome FS	115,000
Boundary Peak FS	10,000
Currant Mountain BLM	3
Currant Mountain FS	36,000
East Humboldts FS	36,900

Grant Range FS	50,000
Jarbidge FS	113,167
Mount Charleston FS	43,000
Mount Moriah BLM	6,435
Mount Moriah FS	70,000
Mount Rose FS	28,000
Quinn Canyon FS	27,000
Ruby Mountains FS	90,000
Santa Rosa-Paradise Peak FS	31,000
Table Mountain FS	98,000
Total Forest Service	
acres in Nevada:	*786,067*
Total Bureau of Land Management	
acres in Nevada:	*6,458*
State Total of Wilderness	
Acreage for Nevada:	*792,525*

New Hampshire

Great Gulf FS	5,552
Pemigewasse FSt	45,000
Presidential Range-Dry River FS	27,380
Sandwich Range FS	25,000
Total Forest Service	
acres in New Hampshire:	*102,932*
State Total of Wilderness	
Acreage for New Hampshire	*102,932*

New Jersey

Brigantine FWS	6,681
Great Swamp FWS	3,660
Total Fish and Wildlife Service	
acres in New Jersey:	*10,341*
State Total of Wilderness Acrege	
for New Jersey:	*10,341*

New Mexico

Aldo Leopold FS	202,016
Apache Kid FS	44,626
Bandelier NPS	23,267
Bisti BLM	3,946
Blue Range FS	29,304
Capitan Mountains FS	34,658
Carlsbad Caverns NPS	33,125
Cebolla BLM	62,800
Chama River Canyon FS	50,300
Chupadera Unit FWS	5,289
Cruces Basin FS	18,000
De-na-zin BLM	22,454
Dome FS	5,200
Gila FS	557,873
Indian Well Unit FWS	5,139
Latir Peak FS	20,000
Little San Pascual Unit FWS	19,859

Manzano Mountain FS — 36,875
Pecos FS — 223,333
Salt Creek FWS — 9,621
San Pedro Parks FS — 41,132
Sandia Mountain FS — 37,877
West Malpais BLM — 39,700
Wheeler Peak FS — 19,661
White Mountain FS — 48,208
Withington FS — 19,000
Total Bureau of Land Management
acres in New Mexico: — *128,900*
Total National Park Service
acres in New Mexico: — *56,392*
Total Forest Service
acres in New Mexico: — *1,388,063*
Total Fish and Wildlife Service
acres in New Mexico — *39,908*
State Total of Wilderness
Acreage for New Mexico: — *1,613,263*

New York
Fire Island NPS — 1,363
Total National Park Service
acres in New York: — *1,363*
State Total of Wilderness
Acreage for New York: — *1,363*

North Carolina
Birkhead Mountains FS — 5,025
Catfish Lake South FS — 8,530
Ellicott Rock FS — 3,394
Joyce Kilmer-Slickrock FS — 13,562
Linville Gorge FS — 11,786
Middle Prong FS — 7,460
Pocosin FS — 11,709
Pond Pine FS — 1,685
Sheep Ridge FS — 9,297
Shining Rock FS — 18,483
Southern Nantahala FS — 11,703
Swanquarter FWS — 8,785
Total Fish and Wildlife Service
acres in North Carolina: — *8,785*
Total Forest Service
acres in North Carolina: — *102,634*
State Total of Wilderness
Acreage for North Carolina — *111,419*

North Dakota
Chase Lake FWS — 4,155
Lostwood FWS — 5,577
Theodore Roosevelt NPS — 29,920
Total Fish and Wildlife Service
acres in North Dakota: — *9,732*

Total National Park Service
acres in North Dakota: — *29,920*
State Total of Wilderness
Acreage for North Dakota: — *39,652*

Ohio
West Sister Island FWS — 77
Total Fish and Wildlife Service
acres in Ohio: — *77*
State Total of Wilderness
Acreage for Ohio: — *77*

Oklahoma
Black Fork Mountain FS — 4,629
Charons Garden Unit FWS — 5,723
North Mountain Unit FWS — 2,847
Upper Kiamichi River FS — 9,802
Total Fish and Wildlife Service
acres in Oklahoma: — *8,570*
Total Forest Service
acres in Oklahoma: — *14,431*
State Total of Wilderness
Acreage for Oklahoma: — *23,001*

Oregon
Badger Creek FS — 24,000
Black Canyon FS — 13,400
Boulder Creek FS — 19,100
Bridge Creek FS — 5,400
Bull of the Woods FS — 34,900
Columbia FS — 39,000
Cummins Creek FS — 9,173
Diamond Peak FS — 54,185
Drift Creek FS — 5,798
Eagle Cap FS — 358,461
Gearhart Mountain FS — 22,809
Grassy Knob FS — 17,200
Hells Canyon BLM — 968
Hells Canyon FS — 130,095
Kalmiopsis FS — 179,655
Menagerie FS — 4,800
Middle Santiam FS — 7,500
Mill Creek FS — 17,400
Monument Rock FS — 19,650
Mount Hood FS — 46,520
Mount Jefferson FS — 107,008
Mount Thielsen FS — 54,267
Mount Washington FS — 52,738
Mountain Lake FS — 23,071
North Fork John Day FS — 121,352
North Fork Umatilla FS — 20,435
Oregon Islands BLM — 5
Oregon Islands FWS — 480

109

Red Buttes FS	3,750
Rock Creek FS	7,486
Rogue-Umpqua Divide FS	33,200
Salmon-Huckleberry FS	44,560
Sky Lakes FS	116,300
Strawberry Mountain FS	68,700
Table Rock BLM	5,750
Three Arch Rocks FWS	15
Three Sisters FS	286,708
Waldo Lake FS	39,200
Wenaha-Tucannon FS	66,375
Wild Rogue FS	25,658
Total Fish and Wildlife Service	
acres in Oregon:	*495*
Total Forest Service	
acres in Oregon:	*2,079,854*
Total Bureau of Land Management	
acres in Oregon	*6,723*
State Total of Wilderness	
Acreage for Oregon:	*2,087,072*

Pennsylvania

Allegheny Islands FS	368
Hickory Creek FS	8,570
Total Forest Service	
acres in Pennsylvania:	*8,938*
State Total of Wilderness	
Acreage for Pennsylvania:	*8,938*

South Carolina

Cape Romain FWS	29,000
Congaree Swamp NPS	15,010
Ellicott Rock FS	2,859
Hell Hole Bay FS	2,125
Little Wambaw Swamp FS	5,047
Wambaw Creek FS	1,825
Wambaw Swamp FS	4,815
Total Forest Service	
acres in South Carolina:	*16,671*
Total National Park Service	
acres in South Carolina:	*15,010*
Total Fish and Wildlife Service	
acres in South Carolina:	*29,000*
State Total of Wilderness	
Acreage for South Carolina:	*60,681*

South Dakota

Badlands NPS	64,250
Black Elk FS	9,826
Total National Park Service	
acres in South Dakota:	*64,250*
Total Forest Service	
acres in South Dakota:	*9,826*

State Total of Wilderness	
Acreage for South Dakota:	*74,076*

Tennessee

Bald River Gorge FS	3,721
Big Frog FS	7,193
Big Laurel Branch FS	6,251
Citico Creek FS	16,226
Cohutta FS	1,709
Gee Creek FS	2,493
Joyce Kilmer-Slickrock FS	3,832
Little Frog Mountain FS	4,666
Pond Mountain FS	6,626
Sampson Mountain FS	7,991
Unaka Mountain FS	4,700
Total Forest Service	
acres in Tennessee:	*65,408*
State Total of Wilderness	
Acreage for Tennessee:	*65,408*

Texas

Big Slough FS	3,455
Guadalupe Mountains NPS	46,850
Indian Mounds FS	10,917
Little Lake Creek FS	3,855
Turkey Hill FS	5,473
Upland Island FS	13,330
Total National Park Service	
acres in Texas:	*46,850*
Total Forest Service	
acres in Texas:	*37,030*
State Total of Wilderness	
Acreage for Texas:	*83,880*

Utah

Ashdown Gorge FS	7,000
Beaver Dam Mountains BLM	3,630
Box-Death Hollow FS	25,751
Dark Canyon FS	45,000
Deseret Peak FS	25,500
High Uintas FS	456,705
Lone Peak FS	30,088
Mount Naomi FS	44,350
Mount Nebo FS	28,000
Mount Olympus FS	16,000
Mount Timpanogos FS	10,750
Paria Canyon-	
Vermilion Cliffs BLM	23,000
Pine Valley Mountain FS	50,000
Twin Peaks FS	11,334
Wellsville Mountain FS	23,850
Total Bureau of Land Management	
acres in Utah:	*26,630*

Total Forest Service	
acres in Utah:	*774,328*
State Total of Wilderness	
Acreage for Utah:	*800,958*

Vermont

Big Branch FS	6,720
Breadloaf FS	21,480
Bristol Cliffs FS	3,738
George D. Aiken FS	5,060
Lye Brook FS	15,503
Peru Peak FS	6,920
Total Forest Service	
acres in Vermont:	*59,421*
State Total of Wilderness	
Acreage for Vermont:	*59,421*

Virginia

Barbours Creek FS	5,700
Beartown FS	5,609
James River Face FS	8,886
Kimberling Creek FS	5,542
Lewis Fork FS	5,618
Little Dry Run FS	2,858
Little Wilson Creek FS	3,613
Mountain Lake FS	8,187
Peters Mountain FS	3,328
Ramseys Draft FS	6,518
Rich Hole FS	6,450
Rough Mountain FS	9,300
Saint Mary's FS	9,835
Shawvers Run FS	3,467
Shenandoah NPS	79,579
Thunder Ridge FS	2,344
Total National Park Service	
acres in Virginia:	*79,579*
Total Forest Service	
acres in Virginia:	*87,255*
State Total of Wilderness	
Acreage for Virginia:	*166,834*

Washington

Alpine Lakes FS	362,621
Boulder River FS	48,674
Buckhorn FS	44,258
Clearwater FS	14,374
Colonel Bob FS	11,961
Glacier Peak FS	572,338
Glacier View FS	3,123
Goat Rocks FS	108,279
Henry M. Jackson FS	99,972
Indian Heaven FS	20,960
Juniper Dunes BLM	6,900

Lake Chelan-Sawtooth FS	151,435
Mount Adams FS	46,626
Mount Baker FS	117,528
Mount Rainier NPS	228,488
Mount Skokomish FS	13,015
Noisy-Diobsud FS	14,133
Norse Peak FS	52,180
Olympic NPS	876,669
Pasayten FS	530,031
Salmo-Priest FS	41,335
San Juan Islands FWS	353
Stephen Mather NPS	634,614
Tatoosh FS	15,750
The Brothers FS	16,682
Trapper Creek FS	5,970
Washington Islands FWS	485
Wenaha-Tucannon FS	111,048
William O. Douglas FS	168,157
Wonder Mountain FS	2,349
Total Fish and Wildlife Service	
acres in Washington:	*838*
Total National Park Service	
acres in Washington:	*1,739,771*
Total Forest Service	
acres in Washington:	*2,572,799*
Total Bureau of Land Management	
acres in Washington:	*6,900*
State Total of Wilderness	
Acreage for Washington:	*4,320,308*

West Virginia

Cranberry FS	35,864
Dolly Sods FS	10,215
Laurel Fork North FS	6,055
Laurel Fork South FS	5,997
Mountain Lake FS	2,721
Otter Creek FS	20,000
Total Forest Service	
acres in West Virginia:	*80,852*
State Total of Wilderness	
Acreage for West Virginia:	*80,852*

Wisconsin

Blackjack Springs FS	5,886
Headwaters FS	18,188
Porcupine Lake FS	4,292
Rainbow Lake FS	6,583
Whisker Lake FS	7,345
Wisconsin Islands FWS	29
Total Fish and Wildlife Service	
acres in Wisconsin:	*29*
Total Forest Service	
acres in Wisconsin:	*42,294*

Wyoming

Absaroka-Beartooth FS	23,283
Bridger FS	428,087
Cloud Peak FS	189,039
Encampment River FS	10,124
Fitzpatrick FS	198,525
Gros Ventre FS	287,000
Huston Park FS	30,588
Jedediah Smith FS	123,451
North Absaroka FS	350,488
Platte River FS	22,749
Popo Agie FS	101,870
Savage Run FS	14,927
Teton FS	585,238
Washakie FS	704,274
Winegar Hole FS	10,715
Total Forest Service	
acres in Wyoming:	*3,080,358*
State Total of Wilderness	
Acreage for Wyoming:	*3,080,358*

National Totals

Total Forest Service	
acres in United States:	*34,676,493*
Total National Park Service	
acres in United States	*43,007,316*
Total Bureau of Land Management	
acres in United States:	*5,227,063*
Total Fish and Wildlife Service	
acres in United States:	*20,685,372*
National Total of Wilderness	
Acreage for All States:	*103,596,244*

Note: Multiple listings are included for those areas designated or affected by more than one public law, managed by more than one agency, located in more than one administrative unit, or located in more than one state.

Source: Bureau of Land Management, Washington, D. C., July 3, 1995.

For further information, contact:
The Wilderness Society
900 17th Street N.W.
Washington, DC 20006

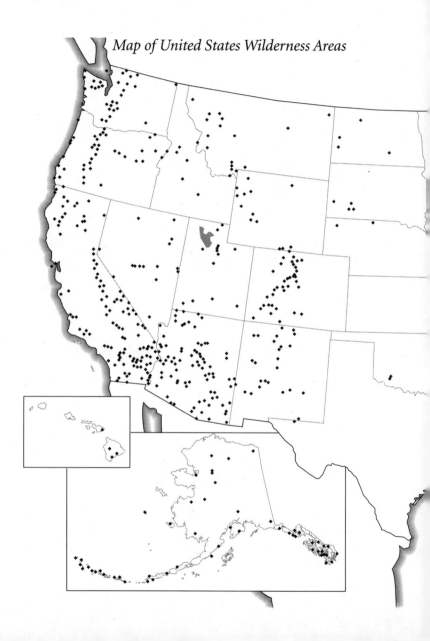

Map of United States Wilderness Areas

Interior design by Will Powers
Typeset in the Minion family
by Stanton Publication Services, Inc.
Printed on recycled, acid-free Glatfelter paper
by Edwards Brothers, Inc.

TESTIMONY PROJECT

Testimony was born out of a desire to influence our leaders through the power of the written word. To continue the use of *Testimony* in this spirit, Milkweed Editions will send a copy of *Testimony* free of charge to your federal or state representative or senator if requested before December 31, 1996.

To send a free copy, please send the following to Milkweed Editions:
- your name and address
- the name of the senator or representative whom you would like to receive *Testimony*, with the appropriate mailing address (if you do not know the address, please indicate the office — state or federal senator or representative)
- your original sales receipt for the book

    Milkweed Editions
    Testimony Project
    430 First Avenue North, Suite 400
    Minneapolis, MN 55401-1743
    FAX: (612) 332-6248

This offer is open only to purchasers of *Testimony* in the United States until December 31, 1996. Only one copy of each book will be sent per copy purchased, and only one copy will be sent to each address along with a letter indicating that the book is being sent on behalf of the original purchaser and including the purchaser's name and address.